W9-AQW-819

TEN LETTER-WRITERS

TEN LETTER-WRITERS

LYN LLOYD IRVINE

Essay Index Reprint Series

BOOKS FOR LIBRARIES PRESS, INC.
FREEPORT, NEW YORK

First Published 1932
Reprinted 1968

LIBRARY OF CONGRESS CATALOG CARD NUMBER:
68-16942

TO

PROFESSOR A. A. JACK

WITH GRATITUDE

CONTENTS

V

CHRONOLOGY

Mme de Sévigné - -	1626–1696
Dorothy Osborne - -	1627–1695
Jonathan Swift - -	1667–1745
Mme du Deffand - -	1697–1780
Horace Walpole - -	1717–1797
William Cowper - -	1731–1800
Lady Bessborough - -	1761–1821
Charles Lamb - -	1775–1834
Mrs. Carlyle - -	1801–1866
Prosper Mérimée - -	1803–1870

ACKNOWLEDGEMENTS

Acknowledgements for kind permission to quote from copyright works are tendered to: His Honour Sir Edward Parry and the Delegates of the Clarendon Press for *The Letters of Dorothy Osborne to William Temple*, edited by Professor G. C. Moore Smith; the Delegates of the Clarendon Press for *The Letters of Horace Walpole*, edited by Mrs. Paget Toynbee ; Messrs. Methuen and Co. Ltd. for *Lettres de Mme du Deffand à Horace Walpole*, edited by Mrs. Paget Toynbee; Messrs. John Lane the Bodley Head Ltd. for *New Letters and Memorials of Jane Welsh Carlyle*, edited by Alexander Carlyle; Messrs. John Murray for *Jane Welsh Carlyle's Letters to her Family*, edited by Leonard Huxley.

I

1. LETTERS AND LITERATURE
2. THE AGE OF LETTER-WRITING
3. WOMEN AS LETTER-WRITERS

I

1. LETTERS AND LITERATURE

LITERATURE on the whole is undated, but letters are firmly set in time and space, their background is definitely and even narrowly geographical and historical. As we read essays or novels we may keep in our minds their century and period, but more as an attribute than as an integral part. Poetry carries the reader into its own timelessness, it is graven on the rock for ever, but letters take him to Florence, to London, to Olney, back to March or June, in 1739 or 1815. Consequently while literature proper loses quickly its association with the pen and paper of the author, it is difficult to think of letters except as material things, placed upon inventories with the old cabinets and boxes in which they are preserved. They may be hoarded sentimentally, as family trinkets are but as literature never is. Dorothy Osborne's letters passed as heirlooms through seven different hands before coming to rest in the British Museum, and they had already passed through six hands before the first extracts from them were published in 1836 in the supplement to Courtenay's *Life and Works of Sir William Temple*. Macaulay admired the extracts in an essay. Judge

Parry read Macaulay's essay and wrote—but not until fifty years later—a sketch of the love affair of Dorothy Osborne which was published in the *English Illustrated Magazine*. There it happened to be read by the sister-in-law of Mr. Robert Bacon Longe of Spixworth Park—the seventh possessor of the letters—and she was moved by the article to make a transcript of the letters, which Judge Parry published in 1888. So by the long-drawn-out linking of coincidences, two hundred and thirty years after Dorothy Osborne became Lady Temple, her love-letters were made public.

Many thousands of letters of interest and merit have had no Macaulay or Judge Parry to deliver them from obscurity. They may have passed into careless hands, or been stolen and hidden, until the moment was ripe for their use by enemies who died with their purposes unfulfilled; they may have been burnt in the Fire of London, put to the uses of waste paper, or appropriated for nests by the philoprogenitive mouse. Some may still lie in the bottoms of old boxes among the family accounts. There are only two or three cases in history where the whole of a famous correspondence has survived. Where are the letters of William Temple to Dorothy Osborne? Where are Stella's letters, where are Lord Granville's, where are Jenny Dacquin's? Lost—no doubt for ever. For without the vanity of a Horace Walpole to direct its fate,[1] almost anything may happen to private correspondence: whereas literature, even when it is the work of genius, finds its

[1] And even his vanity could not be trusted to preserve everything, for his letters to Mme du Deffand have disappeared.

way to the press with the indomitable resource of a land-locked eel making for the open sea. For this reason we read old letters with a little awe and even reverence in our curiosity, as we might listen to the story of a solitary survivor of old adventures. When we meet, as we often do in letters, the commonplaces of history wedged between the trivialities of daily life, they cease to be commonplaces. We feel again the sharpness of the event, the hearts stirred to life or the hearts turned to stone.

" The Duke of Hamilton gave me a pound of snuff to-day, admirable good," wrote Swift to Stella in October 1712. " I wish DD had it and Ppt too, if she likes it. It cost me a quarter of an hour of his politics, which I was forced to hear. Lady Orkney is making me a writing-table of her own contrivance, and a bed nightgown. . . ." So he runs on for a little and ends with a blessing. Here is the next letter to Stella.

" Before this comes to your hands, you will have heard of the most terrible accident that hath almost ever happened. This morning at eight, my man brought me word that Duke Hamilton had fought with Lord Mohun, and killed him, and was brought home wounded. I immediately sent him to the Duke's house, in St. James's Square; but the porter could hardly answer for tears, and a great rabble was about the house. In short they fought at seven this morning. The dog Mohun was killed on the spot; and, while the Duke was over him, Mohun shortening his sword, stabbed him at the shoulder to the heart. The Duke was helped toward the cake-house by the ring in Hyde

Park (where they fought), and died on the grass, before he could reach the house; and was brought home in his coach by eight, while the poor Duchess was asleep."[1]

As well as these differences, the density of the letter, in the sense of the amount of matter per unit of bulk, is not that of literature in general. We must not expect to be amused all the time; we must be prepared to meet with the tediousness and repetitions of life itself. "I do hate," said Mrs. Carlyle, "to tell about myself every day! as if I were the crops." Yet that is just what she must do and what we may expect to find in every correspondence of the best and most natural type. Neither foreshortening nor impressionism can enter in to help us over the details of domestic life and physical ailments and sorrows that even time seems powerless to cure. For fifteen years we follow Mme du Deffand through her sleeplessness almost night by night. The young hate sleep because it robs them of life, and the old hate sleeplessness for just the opposite reason. Each night, said Mme du Deffand, added a year to her age, and since she had not slept for nearly a month she was at least a hundred years old, "avec toutes les circonstances, dépendances, et ornements de ce charmant âge." Sheridan once remarked that although life itself was too short everything in it was too long. So very possibly we feel as we read of Mrs. Carlyle's headaches and Mme du Deffand's sleeplessness and Lord Byron's perpetual need of tooth-powder and Cowper's gratitude for fish. And everything in

[1] *Journal to Stella*, November 15th, 1712.

letters—not only the physical and domestic—has the disproportions of life itself, not the proportions of art. The insight that we get into Cowper's life from reading his letters is something that even the best biography cannot give, and for charm and grace they are scarcely to be matched in English; no one had more skill than he at making stories out of the barest and most trite events of a secluded life. But his collected letters are like a feather bed laid upon the reader feather by feather, each particle alone almost the lightness of air, yet the accumulation of them stifling and insupportable.

2. THE AGE OF LETTER-WRITING

Without drawing too hard a line at either the beginning or the end of the age of letter-writing, it may be said to have opened with the birth of Mme de Sévigné and closed with the death of Mérimée. No century has been better adapted to letter-writing than the eighteenth and none has produced more good letter-writers; the letter expresses the temperament of the eighteenth century as fully as anything that it produced. A cultured, leisured society which extended its franchise—with certain qualifications—to women, a state of material civilisation in which news was hard to gather, postal communication difficult although not by any means impossible, and the telephone unknown—these are obviously the conditions in which letter-writing has thriven. It might thrive again could such an age return.

The universal craving to give and receive news—the ruling passion of the last fifty years—first occupied the attention and services of the educated person of leisure in the seventeenth and eighteenth centuries. Earlier than this, princes, ambassadors and merchants communicated with one another, more or less regularly, and their letters took the place of the modern newspaper. But between friends or the members of a family, except for business purposes and upon occasions of importance, correspondence was rare. Margery Paston did not write to her husband to assure him of her affection or to satisfy any general curiosity about the life of the family in his absence, but as a plain business necessity. " Sir, your mast that lay at Yarmouth is let to a ship of Hull for 13s. 4d., and if there fall any hurt thereto ye shall have a new mast therefore."[1] Partly for practical reasons, partly for psychological, until the second half of the seventeenth century, men and women seldom wrote to their friends in a spirit of idleness and sociability. The attitude of Horace Walpole to letter-writing could scarcely have existed in Tudor England. For the greater part of his life he wrote two or three letters a week, not because he had business to perform with his friends, not because he had vital information to give them, which they could get in no other way, but simply to express his own interest—and satisfy theirs—in the events of his life and the lives of those about him. Some of the events were important, many of them, by Paston or Tudor standards, wholly insignificant. The conception of what constitutes history and of the part played by ordinary people in making and recording it had changed since the sixteenth century. Walpole seems to have realised that as time goes on less and less in man's experience can safely be regarded as trivial. He was fully aware of the importance of his

[1] Margery Paston to John Paston, January 21st, 1486.

correspondence with his friend Sir Horace Mann in Florence. " Well," he wrote in 1771, " as we have closed a long period, pray send me my letters to the end of last year. I believe I have mentioned it once or twice. I should like to have them all together, for they are a kind of history—only think of eight-and-twenty years."[1]

Mérimée, a Walpole of the nineteenth century with a better mind and a far more susceptible heart, had a similar historical interest in the life surrounding him. To tell about it, describe it, note down little scenes and character sketches in one's letters became a habit partly of duty and partly of entertainment. An individual, even by correspondence, could help to prevent this ever-increasing and ever more complicated existence from becoming too unwieldy for the mind to grasp. If a small group of people could keep mental pace with the world, at least within that group there would be comparative ease and freedom from the burden of ignorance, which weighs as heavily on mankind as the burden of sin. For the unknown in life is always chafing the consciousness; it is a wonder that a world which contains eighteen hundred million persons produces no more than thirty or forty thousand newspapers in the endeavour to keep pace with the resulting gossip. Walpole's world, or all of it that concerned an aristocrat, fortunately held nearer eighteen hundred. Mérimée's was larger, but so was his mind.

Letters themselves provide the best record of the conditions that made the eighteenth century so well

[1] Horace Walpole to Sir Horace Mann, January 15th, 1771.

suited for the writing of them, and the best record of the changes which the nineteenth century introduced. It is in letters that many of the most significant factors of common life, overlooked by the professional historian, receive the attention due to them. The reader of letters observes that as the eighteenth century passes, smallpox and gout cease to be mentioned, influenza and lumbago take their places. In December 1805 Lady Bessborough writes to Lord Granville, who was then on his way to Russia: "Everybody is dying with violent coughs and colds—they call it influenza; whatever it is, I have got it, tho' not so bad as my poor Caro,[1] who has been again blooded. . . ." Thirty years later influenza has grown familiar. "Dear M.," wrote Lamb to Moxon in 1833, "Mary and I are very poorly. Ashbury says 'tis nothing but influenza. . . . My bedfellows are Cough and cramp, we sleep 3 in a bed." The generations that have suffered from influenza belong to the same household as ourselves; cough and cramp have been our bedfellows too; we live in the age of both newspapers and influenza.

Earlier than the seventeenth and eighteenth centuries, in addition to the hindrances to good letter-writing due to lack of education, particularly among women, and the difficulties of communication by post, there existed a psychological deterrent. Men and women had not acquired the habit of talking freely about themselves. They did not even think freely about themselves, according to modern standards.

[1] Her daughter, Lady Caroline Ponsonby (afterwards Lamb).

Even between Dorothy Osborne and Mrs. Carlyle we can measure a wide difference.[1] Although Dorothy Osborne wrote to her lover, she erred on the side of reserve; while Mrs. Carlyle erred in the opposite direction, no matter to whom she wrote. Freedom of self-expression gone to extremes probably had as much to do with the passing of the golden age of letter-writing as did the telephone and the penny post. It is easier to row well against the current, and to write well when the conventions demand certain slight restrictions upon speech.

Walpole addressed Mann with an odd formality and severity, asking for his letters—" I believe I have mentioned it once or twice "—he spoke as a clerk anxious to keep his files in order. Very different was the attitude of his friend Mme du Deffand to letter-writing.

" Je vous prie seulement de me tenir parole, de m'écrire avec la plus grande confiance, et d'être persuadé que je suis plus à vous qu'à moi-même. Je vous rendrai compte, de mon côté, de tout ce qui me regarde, et je causerai avec vous comme si nous étions tête-à-tête au coin du feu."[2]

Mérimée, although upon his intellectual side he shared and developed many of Walpole's characteristics, appreciated almost as fully as Mme du Deffand the peculiar freedom, egotism and simplicity permitted, ideally, in letter-writing. He delighted in the

[1] Mr. Leonard Woolf, in *After the Deluge* (pp. 242-8), gives an extremely interesting outline of the effect upon literature of " this curious psychological revolution."

[2] Mme du Deffand to Horace Walpole, April 19th, 1766.

intimacy and absence of restraint—no need for excuses or explanations, no need to qualify generalisations or to soften criticisms.

Mme du Deffand's understanding of the foundation for a satisfactory correspondence was essentially that of a woman. Letters are in many ways women's affair, so much so that one could select ten letter-writers, from Mme de Sévigné to Mrs. Carlyle, all either women or, like Cowper, so feminine in their letters that one can fairly group them with women. But lest this short survey should be open to an accusation of favouring either sex, two of the ten chosen are contrasting males, Swift and Lamb, letter-writers indubitably of the first rank, yet as surely masculine. They prove their masculinity by the way they take their ease in letters. While the feminine letter-writer seeks her relaxation in confession and self-revelation, the masculine seeks his in the play of humour and invention. There is no such thing as a foolish sex and a sensible one, yet a serious man will often find relief in some form of entertainment entirely unconnected with seriousness, while a serious woman seldom does. She prefers the change to another type of seriousness. Letters gave Swift and Lamb a welcome opportunity for rank foolishness, some of it of a type which dates them as belonging to another era than ours. For the idea of the humorous has developed along the more sophisticated lines followed by Cowper or Mérimée or Mrs. Carlyle, and the humour of modern times is more feminine than that of the Elizabethans, or of their direct descendants, Swift and Lamb.

But while I have divided my ten letter-writers into three groups—the letter-historians (in II), with Mme du Deffand inevitably linked to them; the feminine letter-writers, who are the heart of the matter (in III and IV); and finally the jesters, the males (in V)—there are two characteristics which are common to all ten. Letter-writers are almost always likeable, partly no doubt because through letters is an attractive way in which to approach any character. In one sense or another many people are mad to the court of Denmark but sane to Horatio. Lady Bessborough to Lord Granville, the Byron of the letters to Moore and Murray and Lady Melbourne, Swift to Stella—there can be no question of the reality and sincerity of this Lady Bessborough, this Byron and this Swift.[1] Nevertheless the freshness and health of their letter-lives do not tally with the opinions which the outer world held of them, opinions hard to ignore. But even making allowances for the fact that one sees them in favourable conditions, letter-writers are distinguished from the bulk of humanity by generosity and affection. In a sense these virtues are theirs by definition, for lacking them few men or women would expend their time and energy in an occupation without remuneration, without—normally—any promise of contemporary or posthumous fame, without even the certainty of receiving, through the replies to their letters, a pleasure equal to that which they were bestowing. A

[1] For instance, what a perfect shot Byron aimed at the popular idea of himself, when, on being taxed by Murray with a fresh seduction, he replied, " I—who have been more ravished than anyone since the siege of Troy."

taste for conversation often indicates an agreeable and friendly nature, but not necessarily an ardent or unselfish one, while the letter-writer is almost necessarily inspired either by altruism or love, often by both. Nor does an unintelligent, material love seek expression in letters, but only such love as physical separation cannot discourage. Certainly there have been letters in which sex played little or no part—in this book those of Walpole, Cowper and Lamb—but over a wider field the proportion of letters in which love was not the main theme would probably be smaller.[1]

The other general characteristic of the letter-writer is the even, established tenor of his existence. None of these ten people was either very active or very adventurous. Their ideas of what was essential for comfort and contentment were on the whole high, for Mme de Sévigné, Dorothy Osborne, Walpole, Mme du Deffand and Lady Bessborough lived within the aristocratic circle; Swift and Mérimée, by virtue of their wits, on the fringe of it, and only Cowper, Lamb and Mrs. Carlyle were definitely of the middle classes. The letter in its heyday was indeed largely the monopoly of the aristocracy. Thus the life and thought reflected in it has rarely been characterised by anxiety or marked by any grave vicissitudes. This requires some emphasis here since in the following pages the reader will find comparatively little retelling of what actually happened.

[1] Although most of Mme de Sévigné's letters were to her daughter, she obviously made her affection for her daughter the outlet for a disposition excessively "temperamental," although perhaps not normally so. See p. 113.

The biographies of most letter-writers are dominated by personality rather than events, and in this book the discussion naturally centres upon the personality, except where—as in the case of Lady Bessborough—the best approach to it seemed to be through a history of events.

3. WOMEN AS LETTER-WRITERS

" And first let mee aske you if you have seen a book of Poems newly come out, made by my Lady New Castle. for God sake if you meet with it send it mee, they say t'is ten times more Extravagant than her dresse. Sure the poore woman is a little distracted, she could never be soe rediculous else as to venture at writeing book's and in verse too. If I should not sleep this fortnight I should not come to that."[1]

It is hard to believe that Dorothy Osborne, with her clear independent mind, was merely echoing public opinion when she wrote this. She was a reader of many books, a " devote " of Jeremy Taylor's and a stylist herself, but yet felt that it was not in her to write, and could not understand its being in any woman. Walpole wishing to give Mme du Deffand another interest in life asked her why she always read, why she did not write—it would be more amusing—she could write about the things she had seen. Her reply was precise and conclusive. She said that she had neither the taste nor the talent for writing, and could do it only when she had a particular object in view—to

[1] Dorothy Osborne to William Temple, April 14th, 1653.

write in cold blood was impossible and the past was so nearly blotted out that unless she were questioned she remembered none of it.[1] Neither in her reasons nor in the comments of Dorothy Osborne on Lady Newcastle can one trace self-depreciation or affected modesty. The excuse is not lack of ability so much as lack of disposition. Still less—as one would imagine—did Mrs. Carlyle suffer from a sense of intellectual inferiority; a favourite target for her sarcasm was the commonplace view of women. " Well," she wrote to John Sterling, after opening her letter with a succinct and lively account of John Forster, " Well! all this preamble was not essential to the understanding of what is to follow; but at least it will not help to darken it, which is as much as could be expected of a female writer."[2] When Chapman and Hall offered her good terms for a novel if she would write one, she did not consider the suggestion either " extravagant " or " rediculous," but no novel was written; she got no nearer to the task than considering how good a subject her mysterious neighbours at 6 Cheyne Row would make—the owner of the stunning cock and nine hens and the little boy too excitable to go to school.

Neither Mme de Sévigné nor Mme du Deffand nor Lady Bessborough nor Mrs. Carlyle took the prompting to write letters lightly or idly, but it was an avocation that demanded none of the application necessary for a set task. A letter can be begun and ended as the mood dictates, written in a sick-room or in a crowd of

[1] Mme du Deffand to Horace Walpole, March 11th, 1772.
[2] Mrs. Carlyle to John Sterling, January 19th, 1842.

company, and the inspiration is given and renewed perpetually by the demands of friendship and by the desire to give pleasure where one loves. The conscious and unswerving intention of the artist, so individual and so rarely communicated or shared, differs in root and branch from the mood of the letter-writer. Whatever may be true of the present and the future, it is at least true of the past that women have often felt the inspiration to write letters and seldom the inspiration to write books. The great legal theme of literature, the Job theme, lying behind all tragedies, accords little with their natures—not because women imagine the world justly ordered, but because they are too familiar with injustice. The active enemies of slavery are the free or the partially free, not the slaves themselves. Even when women have undertaken creative work they evade the greater issues, the question of good and evil in the universe, the statement of man's case against the gods. George Eliot it is true dealt with such things: "Somehow I cannot relish her," said Fitzgerald. There seems to remain in women a core of indifference about the fate of the universe—due perhaps to the anodyne of sensual consolations—and counterbalancing it, intense concern for the fate of anyone near, a child, a lover. But all that concerns the sexes as emotionally different must be speculation; men in discussing such things are hampered because they do not know what it is to be a woman, and women because they do not know what it is to be anything else.

Moreover, the impulse towards literary creation is unpractical and spiritual, while women are practical and rarely spiritual. The practical aspect of letter-writing, its value in expressing and encouraging affection between parents and children, or between lovers, has made it an occupation to which women were naturally drawn. Spirituality and piety are sometimes closely connected, but while piety may develop out of spirituality, it is rare for the reverse to happen. Of the five women letter-writers in this book the least feminine and the most sceptical was also the most spiritual—Mme du Deffand. Dorothy Osborne, Mme de Sévigné, Lady Bessborough and Mrs. Carlyle, absorbed in lives of affection and small practical concerns, were all inclined to a conventional moderate piety. Let Mme de Sévigné, most lucid and ready of catechumens, answer her daughter's question as to whether she is " dévote."

" Vous me demandez si je suis dévote; hélas! non, dont je suis trés-fachée; mais il me semble que je me détache en quelque sorte de ce qui s'appelle le monde. La vieillesse et un peu de maladie donnent le temps de faire de grandes réflexions. . . ."[1]

At another time she wrote:

" Une de mes grandes envies, c'est d'être dévote; j'en tourmente tous les jours la Mousse.[2] Je ne suis ni à Dieu, ni au diable: cet état m'ennuie, quoiqu'entre nous je le trouve le plus naturel du monde."[3]

Lady Bessborough—except when Lord Granville was in the cabinet and she found herself repeating the

[1] Mme de Sévigne to Mme de Grignan, June 8th, 1676.
[2] L'Abbé Pierre de la Mousse.
[3] Mme de Sévigné to Mme de Grignan, June 10th, 1671.

state prayers with fervency—and Mrs. Carlyle—except when her dog Nero died and a verse or two in Romans held out hope of the immortality of animals—might both have put their names to this avowal, that they belonged neither to God nor the Devil and found it the most natural state in the world. But Mme du Deffand, agnostic from her childhood, could not pretend to find agnosticism the most natural state in the world. " *Croyez*, dit-on, *c'est le plus sur ;* mais comment croit-on ce que l'on ne comprend pas? . . . Je suis comme un sourd et un aveugle-né; il y a de sons, des couleurs, il en convient; mais sait-il de quoi il convient? "[1] She must consult a true friend before packing up to leave this world, for she was parched for lack of belief, destitute of an acceptable theory of life after death. Unorthodoxy is a severe master; those who serve him as faithfully as Mme du Deffand follow a narrow and stony track of thought. The pliable orthodoxy of Mme de Sévigné or Lady Bessborough sets the mind free to range and relieves it of some of the heaviest of human fears. Mrs. Carlyle had her doubts about Christianity; " Love? " she wrote once, " It isn't much like a world ruled by love, this." But she was too nervous and erratic to dispense with religion on rational grounds if she could obtain any solace from it. She kept it by her, as she did morphia. Dorothy Osborne took a sterner, more consistent view of religion; she could not have admitted easily that she belonged to neither God nor the Devil; indeed she inclined to asceticism and believed it was wrong to

[1] Mme du Deffand to Horace Walpole, April 1st, 1769.

desire with passion any earthly pleasure, believed that the strength of her feeling for Temple—to us so exquisitely restrained and modest—ought to have been a thing " fear'd and shunn'd." She and her brother Henry discussed religion like " two hermitts . . . in a Cell they equally inhabitt," and when matters were in a critical way between her and Temple, she begged him not to upset her by his letters until after Christmas, " for to deale freely wth you," she said, " I have some devotions to perform wch must not be disturbed with any thing." But in this as in all her ways she was not so much possessed by a spiritual idea as seeking by a rule of life half Stoic, half Christian, to teach herself indifference to the disappointments and trials of this world, and serene endurance of its sorrows. " When wee have tryed all wayes to happiness, there is noe such thing to bee found, but in a minde conformed to on's condition whatsoever it bee, and in not aymeing at any things that is either imposible, or improbable; all the rest is but Vanity and Vexation of Spirritt, and I durst pronounce it soe from that litle knowledge I have had of the world though I had not Scripture for my warrant."[1]

Contentment was everything and if she were denied the three things—" a True friend, a moderate fortune, and a retired life "—in which contentment consisted, then she would set about conforming her mind to her condition " whatsoever it bee."

Women, then, generally speaking, and with a few exceptions admitted, are less creative and imaginative

[1] Dorothy Osborne to William Temple, December 8th-10th, 1653.

writers than men, their scope is smaller, they are practical, adaptable, seldom spiritual, seldom purposive. That these limitations are no disadvantage to a letter-writer but actually an advantage scarcely needs to be said, and it is clear enough why so many women with no literary ambition or pretensions should enjoy letter-writing and should do it well. But within the high walls of these limitations the feminine letter-writer makes her own excursions in imagination and discovers her own ways of escaping from the present and the physical and the " little things " that are always threatening to eat her up. She undergoes a temporary metamorphosis; the self divides into two, one person observes and records, the other acts and feels and is observed, and both escape—for the moment—from the vexations and tedium of existence. For the observing self sees but does not suffer the emotional drama, and the observed self, robbed as it were of mind, suffers mildly and patiently, like a wounded animal. It is an imaginative gift particularly feminine, although the archetype of all who have fostered it in themselves is Shakespeare's *Richard II*. Romance and the sentimental combine—events are seen as though at a distance, and appear strange, with the charm of a life not belonging to the liver of it, and the emotions are nursed and protected by a passing illusion. Mme du Deffand consoled herself as little by such means as Jane Austen amused herself by them, but in Lady Bessborough's letters and in Mrs. Carlyle's there is plenty of evidence of the imaginative duality. Here are two short scenes from Lady Bessborough where, with a foreshadowing of the Brontë fashion in her sympathetic use of darkness and wild weather, she describes herself with just a trace of conscious poignancy, proving that she is a little detached, as she regards her own unhappiness.

"I was in the bedroom, and I heard somebody play a few notes on the piano forte. Oh G., *mi palpita il cuore*; how often have I flown at that call. I cannot tell you the feel it gave me. Candles were not brought, and as I push'd the door open I only saw the tall figure of a Man, which tho' very unlike you in fact, seen so and at that time, made an impression on me I could not recover the whole night."[1]

"I came here yesterday; the wind blew loud against my windows and whistled thro' the old casements, and prevent'd my sleeping. I also sat up reading some letters my mother gave me, written many years ago, in a hand writing[2] I can never see without the keenest emotions of tenderness and regret. . . ."[3]

These tides of emotion were welcome, clearly; she did not resent the tender memories—the harrow passed over the heart of the dream personality, and she experienced almost the catharsis of one watching a play which depicted sorrows like her own but not hers. When Mrs. Carlyle wrote to Dr. Carlyle, describing her secret and ghostly visit to Haddington, her first return in twenty years, when she found that some

[1] Lady Bessborough to Lord Granville, February 24th, 1805. From *The Private Correspondence of Lord Granville Leveson Gower 1781-1821*, (John Murray).

[2] That of the Duchess of Devonshire, then dead.

[3] Lady Bessborough to Lord Granville, December 4th, 1806.

unknown person had recently cleaned the first two lines on her father's tombstone, and herself cleaned the rest with his own pearl-handled button-hook, returning to the task so early in the morning that she had to climb the wall of the churchyard—she did not resent her feelings. " It was a sorrow more satisfactory to me than any pleasures could be at this date," she wrote.[1]

The melancholy of Dorothy Osborne is far more single-hearted; whenever she speaks of her own unhappiness she leaves us in little doubt that she has not succeeded in romanticising it away. " Tis a sad thing when all on's happinesse is only that ye world dos not know you are miserable." " God know's I am an inconsiderable person born to a thousand misfortun's which have taken away all sence of anything else from mee and left mee a walking missery only." It is only in her less unhappy moments that she has the detachment to see herself and make a vignette—in the garden until eleven at night—" the Jessomine smelt beyond all perfumes, and yet I was not pleased."[2]

What finally of Mme de Sévigné—was she romantic or realist? Compared with Lady Bessborough, she may look like a realist, and certainly she never indulged in anything nearer to self-romanticising than complacent observation of the docility of her spirit. But she had no need to pick out herself as a romantic subject, since she saw the entire universe romantically. Providence was her hero, the ways of providence a drama which she

[1] Mrs. Carlyle to Dr. Carlyle, July 28th, 1849. Or for a much fuller record of the same visit, see *Letters and Memorials of J. W. C.*, Vol. II, pp. 53-65.

[2] Dorothy Osborne to William Temple, July 16th, 1653.

watched with perpetual satisfaction; probably no one has ever seen life more nearly perfect than she did. But for that she had to juggle with facts and the juggling habit is hers as clearly as it is not Mme du Deffand's. "Vous me paroissez folle de votre fils," she wrote to her daughter once, "j'en suis fort aise. On ne sauroit avoir trop de fantaisies, musquées ou point musquées, il n'importe."[1]

There are minds capable of immense labour so long as they are not confronted at the outset by the need to conceive it in its entirety. Such minds produced the eight hundred letters of Mme du Deffand to Horace Walpole and the thirteen volumes of Mme de Sévigné's correspondence. Patience in one of its aspects is a necessity in creation, but there are two kinds of patience, one which knowingly undertakes a pyramid or *The Decline and Fall of the Roman Empire* and the other which is merely a disposition to permit life to take its way. Good letter-writers as a rule possess only the second kind and women letter-writers particularly seem to lack the first. Whether through tradition or by nature women in everything show more submission than initiative; they are either resigned to life's "contrariety's" or confident in the ways of providence. They have more resilience than men and bear pain better—so it is said—but they lack the patience necessary to enterprise. Living less individually than men, they distrust what is novel and strange, they admire the achievement of the past, but question that of the future. Even in favourable circumstances

[1] Mme de Sévigné to Mme de Grignan, January 20th, 1672.

they show a reluctance to undertake creation and invention, which is often not justified by a lack of talent and imagination and only partially explained by public discouragement.

But to suggest that women lack creative energy and the disposition to make the same uses of their talents as men, is not to accuse them of indolence. The infinite capacity for taking pains which forms at least a part of genius—that is feminine enough. Impossible to deny its possession to Lady Bessborough as she ransacked her memory for news for Lord Granville; or to Mme du Deffand cherishing for Horace Walpole every morsel of Paris gossip; or to Mrs. Carlyle even in illness gleaning her sheaf of comedy from the day's irritations; or to Mme de Sévigné dispensing her wit *en pièces de quatre sols* which she had amassed with miserly pleasure and care. In each case the stimulus was exactly what each required, not the admiration of the world, not even the expectation of posthumous fame, but the undelayed, intimate response of a loved person.

The same stimulus indeed was what Mérimée required, and Cowper, and men have written as admirable letters as women on countless occasions. Nevertheless—with a few exceptions—the more masculine the character of the male letter-writer, the less distinct as a rule his genius for letter-writing. But it is time that the stigma attached to the term "feminine" should be removed. No indignity has been done to Cowper by placing him in the same group as Lady Bessborough and Mrs. Carlyle; the femininity of his letters is their beauty. " Feminine " applied to literature defines a type of work as capable of perfection as any other. As to the relative values of the different types, that is a matter over which it requires more courage to dogmatise than the average critic possesses. It is safest not to give the perfect sonnet higher marks than the perfect comedy or to place the best novelist above the best letter-writer. Let us judge the specimens in the literary exhibition in their classes and according to the merits of their type. Here ten letter-writers are displayed, choice examples of their kind.

II

1. WALPOLE
2. WALPOLE AND MME DU DEFFAND
3. MME DU DEFFAND
4. MÉRIMÉE

II

1. WALPOLE

SINCE Walpole is generally considered the best English letter-writer he falls naturally into the first place. But although he may have been the best he is by no means typical, and some of his marked characteristics are of a kind rarely found among good letter-writers. He was reserved and afraid of what even his intimate friends might think of him if he opened his heart too freely to them. And although he was vain—perhaps because he was vain—he did not take much interest in his own personality. Nine times out of ten the attraction of a volume of letters lies in the frank expression of the writer's feelings and the free revelation of character, while the general information which the letters may contain possesses secondary importance. In Walpole's letters all this is reversed. We read him for what he tells us, not for what he is.

He had a great deal to tell, for he never wasted himself in work, but employed all his energies in watching people and listening to them, and reporting all that he saw and heard to his friends. Consequently his letters lay clear the whole life of a century.

His life was long—he was born in 1717 and died in

1797—and he preserved until the very end of it the curiosity about people and events and the appetite for gossip which he had developed in the early twenties. By his taste for friendships with those much younger and much older than himself, he evaded some of the limitations of mortality. Through two women in particular he succeeded in artificially extending his four score years until they seem to us nearer six score. The figure of Walpole—a slight, rather dandified man with a " highly gentlemanly " voice, who walked "as if afraid of a wet floor," tripping like a peewit (he said himself) in his best days, and afterwards " more like a dabchick "—throws its elongated shadow over the whole eighteenth century, and even over parts of the seventeenth and the nineteenth.

At forty-eight he made the acquaintance of Mme du Deffand, nearly twenty years his senior, and mistress in her youth to the Regent, Philippe d'Orléans, who when he put on a ruff looked like his grandfather Henri IV, only more handsome. The life thus linked up with the last dregs of the Renascence was also linked to the democracy and domesticity of the nineteenth century. Mary Berry, the intimate friend of Walpole's last years, had been born only a few years before Mme du Deffand died, and lived to edit her letters, picking the brains of Bishop Rodez, a Revolution *émigré* who had known her. She even lived to quarrel with Macaulay because he called Walpole artificial and capricious, and for the last fifteen years of her life Queen Victoria sat upon the throne. But different as Mme du Deffand and Mary Berry were, and wide as the gap is between the Regent and Queen Victoria, these two women had in common something that particularly endeared them to Walpole. Mme du Deffand's blindness left her no amusement but conversation, and Mary Berry and her sister were renowned for their ability to talk intelligently on any subject.

While Walpole used his friendships to stake a claim in the past and the future, he also used them to extend his knowledge of life and affairs beyond the English Channel. Through Mme du Deffand he came into touch and kept in touch with many of the most notable of his French contemporaries. Voltaire would have liked to enter the lists against him over the question of the relative merits of Shakespeare and Racine, but Walpole's natural timidity and the advice of his friends in France (also friends of Voltaire, unwilling to be drawn into a contest that might lose them either Voltaire or Walpole or both) unfortunately prevented what might have been one of the most entertaining disputes of the century. For while Voltaire was an almost unparalleled duellist, Walpole, whose taste upon lesser matters often went astray, admired Shakespeare with knowledge, discrimination and fervour in almost equal parts. It infuriated him that French criticism had succeeded in ousting the gravediggers from *Hamlet*. Besides the nervous flirtation with Voltaire, Walpole distinguished himself and won European fame by baiting Jean-Jacques Rousseau. His intention was merely to make fun of Rousseau privately among his friends, but the letter was copied, got about, was thought by Rousseau to be the work of D'Alembert and Hume, and caused a breach between Rousseau and Hume. The waves of disturbance were even more out of proportion to the pebble that originated them than is usually the case. And as another, more striking testimony to Walpole's cosmopolitanism, the Duc de Choiseul, Louis XV's minister, wished him to be English Ambassador at Paris. But earlier than this, by his grand tour at the age of twenty-two, he had thrown his net still further into the sea of European politics and had formed a friendship with Horace Mann, the English Ambassador at Florence. For forty years, without ever meeting again, they corresponded regularly, and Mann, bore though he was, could at least keep Walpole informed upon the less subtle aspects of transalpine affairs.

Such was, briefly, Walpole's span as a letter-writer, chronologically and geographically. If we wish to consider also his quality as a historian, we cannot do better than examine his " Reminiscences written . . . in 1788 for the amusement of Miss Mary and Miss Agnes Berry." Anyone who has found selections of his letters unsatisfactory and the eighteen volumes of Mrs. Paget Toynbee's edition intimidating, would be well advised to acquire the taste for Walpole's epistolary manner and material through the Reminiscences. There history presents itself in its most entertaining guise, hovering between matters of public interest and private curiosity, scandalous but never trivial, and studded with fragments of real speech and real behaviour. Sir Robert Walpole had ruined Mr.

Pulteney's parliamentary prospects by arranging that he should be offered an earldom—knowing that his vanity would prevent him from seeing the trap until too late. Horace had never forgotten his father's satisfaction upon the success of the stratagem. " I remember my Father's action when he returned from court and told me what he had done, ' I have turned the key of the closet on him,' making that motion with his hand."

For these Reminiscences Walpole relied partly upon his own memories, partly upon those of Lady Suffolk, Pope's Chloe, formerly George II's mistress, and in her old age and retirement at Twickenham, Walpole's neighbour and gossip. One can easily understand his friendship with the deaf old lady, who had been so decorous all her life and profited so little by her fifteen years as the king's mistress that she was "always treated as if her virtue had never been questioned; her friends even affecting to suppose that her connection with the King had been confined to pure friendship." The eighteenth century indulged in compromises just as readily as the nineteenth, and the blend of irregularity and discretion was just what Walpole could understand and appreciate. He even more than Lady Suffolk proved " content to dwell in Decencies for ever," and in his domestic habits he was a match for any old woman of either century. Extremely abstemious, fond of " comfortable tea and bread and butter," he was never addicted to exercise, but interested in " bootikins " to ward off gout, and a firm believer in Dr. James's powders.

Both Walpole and Lady Suffolk had had particularly good opportunities of knowing the court and the aristocracy of the early eighteenth century and " each was eager to learn what either could relate more; and thus by comparing notes, we sometimes could make out discoveries of a third circumstance, before unknown to both." Walpole had unusual advantages in describing the life of his time: he not only possessed knowledge of individual characters, and was aided by vanity to dissect them and by malice to describe them, but he knew—from his upbringing and his interest in the past—the characteristics of the families to which each individual belonged. In 1764 writing to the Earl of Hertford he said: " Yorke would have taken the Rolls, if they would have made it much more considerable, but as they would not, he has recollected that it would be clever for one Yorke to have the air of being disinterested, so he only disgraces himself, and takes a patent of precedence over the Solicitor-General. . . ."[1]

When Walpole first knew Mme du Deffand he cultivated her for the same purpose that he had cultivated Lady Suffolk. He did not like her followers and he sometimes found her conversation coarse, but as soon as he could get her fifty years back (he wrote to Selwyn) she was delicious, and he could put up with anything for the sake of the Regent. A great part of Walpole's life was given up to the study and admiration of " fifty years back "; the young and fragile son of a man of immense vigour and importance, he lived

[1] Horace Walpole to the Earl of Hertford, December 3rd, 1764.

in the shadow of his great father, and it was inevitable that the times of his father should seem to him greater than his own.[1]

But his interest in the present was scarcely less acute. He prided himself on never being without news, and with purveying it to his friends "piping-hot as it comes from the bakers."

"You see," he wrote to Mary Berry in 1793—after giving her all the news that he could gather—"you see how I labour in your service, though my crops are small. An old Duchess of Rutland, mother of the late Duchess of Montrose, whenever a visitor told her some news or scandal, cried to her daughter 'Lucy, do step into the next room, and make a memorandum of what Lady Greenwich, or Lady M. M. or N. N. has been telling us.' 'Lord! Madam, to be sure it cannot be true.' 'No matter, child; it will do for news into the country.' It is for want of such prudent *provision pour le couvent*, that so many people are forced to invent offhand. You cannot say I am so thoughtless. . . ."[2]

Unfortunately Walpole never extended his liking and curiosity to the literary world of his time. His friendship with Gray did not necessitate any entrance into it, and of Johnson he could scarcely have been less appreciative than he was, always referring to him with pettish disapproval. Dr. Johnson's antipathies made

[1] For Walpole's admiration of his father, see his letter to Sir Horace Mann, January 13th, 1780: ". . . O, my father! twenty years of peace, and credit and happiness, and liberty . . . a man who in twenty years never attempted a stretch of power, did nothing but the common business of administration, and by that temperance and steady virtue, and unalterable good humour and superior wisdom, baffled all the efforts faction. . . ."

[2] Horace Walpole to Mary Berry, October 7th, 1793.

him an easy target for his enemies but to-day Walpole's sympathies make him the more ridiculous of the two. His errors of taste were endless; they shocked Mme du Deffand profoundly. "Ah! mon Dieu, mon Dieu, il faut que mon goût pour vous soit à toute épreuve, pour en conserver après les aveux que vous me faites! Aimer Crébillon, et nommément l' *Écumoire!*"[1] Walpole found Fielding too virile and Richardson too middle-class, and the *Journal to Stella* "childish vulgar stuff." Whenever he disliked anything, he showed the smallness and weakness of his nature. In a letter to Mason written in January 1781 occurs an unforgettable description of a conversation between Walpole and Gibbon, who had just lent him the second volume of *The Decline and Fall.* Walpole told Gibbon that he had "pitched on so disgusting a subject" that he feared "few will have patience to read it." On hearing this, Gibbon, said Walpole, "coloured; all his round features squeezed themselves into sharp angles; he screwed up his button-mouth, and rapping his snuff-box, said 'It had never been put together before'—*so well* he meant to add—but gulped it." Gibbon, not unnaturally, ceased to call and did not trouble to send Walpole the third volume. "So much for literature and its fops," said Walpole.[2]

His attitude to literature had its origin partly in

[1] Mme du Deffand to Horace Walpole, March 9th, 1777.

[2] Walpole had few opinions which he did not live to change. In 1789 he wrote to Lady Ossory: "Mr. Gibbon never tires me." Again, also in 1789: "I am a little surprised, I confess, at your Ladyship's finding it laborious to finish Mr. Gibbon, especially the last volume, which I own, too, delighted me the most."

snobbishness, a distaste to be associated even indirectly with Grub Street, but partly in a much more curious cast in his nature. For the arts he had the distrust of the early Roman. Although he despised Seneca, he must have absorbed many of his maxims through the middleman-service of Bacon, and he adopted early something of the Roman attitude towards his family, his friends, the state, art and his own life. It showed itself in his comment to Lady Ossory upon Garrick's funeral. " Yes, Madam, I do think the pomp of Garrick's funeral perfectly ridiculous. It is confounding the immense space between pleasing talents and national services. What distinctions remain for a patriot hero, when the most solemn have been showered on a player?—but when a great empire is on its decline, one symptom is, there being more eagerness on trifles than on essential objects."[1] Garrick's funeral, one must remember in fairness to Walpole, erred on the side of ostentation and expensiveness, but one's sympathy goes to the undertaker not paid three years after Garrick's death, and ruined, rather than to the " patriot hero " defrauded of posthumous glory. But patriotic fervour was not infrequently diluted with a little cynicism, for Walpole was always afraid of making a fool of himself. To Sir Horace Mann he wrote in 1773: " What is England now?—a sink of Indian wealth, filled in by nabobs and emptied by Maccaronis! A senate old and despised! A country overrun by horse-racers! A gaming, robbing, wrangling, railing nation, without principles, genius, charac-

[1] Horace Walpole to the Countess of Upper Ossory, February 1st, 1779.

ter, or allies; the overgrown shadow of what it was! Lord bless me! I run on like a political barber. . . ."[1]

Yet Walpole possessed none of the hardiness and masculine firmness that one associates with the Roman patrician. Mme du Deffand once praised his courage and elicited an unqualified denial from him. "Je suis colère et timide; je n'ai aucune presence d'esprit; il me faut du temps pour me calmer et pour me donner de jugement. Je suis bien petit à mes propres yeux. Je fais le fier mal à propos, le souple avec plus mauvaise grâce encore. . . ." His natural timidity and his civilisation come out in a disgust for "the carnage line of business." To Henry Seymour Conway he wrote: "In spite of you, and all the old barons our ancestors, I pray that we may have done with glory, and would willingly burn every Roman and Greek historian who have done nothing but transmit precedents for cutting throats."[2] And in a similar vein he poured ridicule upon the idea of Empire.

"Who but Machiavel can pretend that we have a shadow of title to a foot of land in India; unless, as our law deems that what is done extra-parochially is deemed to have happened in the parish of St. Martin's-in-the-Fields, India must in course belong to the crown of Great Britain? Alexander distrained the goods and chattels of Porus upon a similar plea; and the popes thought all the world belonged to them, as heirs-at-law

[1] Horace Walpole to Sir Horace Mann, July 13th, 1773.

[2] Horace Walpole to the Hon. Henry Seymour Conway, September 25th, 1761.

to One who had not an acre upon earth. We condemned and attainted the popes without trial, which was not in fashion in the reign of Henry the Eighth, and, by the law of forfeiture, confiscated all their injustice to our own use; and thus, till we shall be ejected, have we a right to exercise all the tyranny and rapine that ever was practised by any of our predecessors anywhere,—as it was in the beginning, is now, and ever shall be, world without end."[1]

Except for a phrase or two it might be Mr. Aldous Huxley, and if Walpole wrote to Mme du Deffand in the lost letters with this mixture of common sense and exaggeration, her high admiration for his mind and his wit is less puzzling.

But leaving such contradictions aside for the moment and returning to the Roman in him, he not only distrusted the arts and put the patriot hero above the genius, but he distrusted and suppressed the emotions; he congratulated himself upon his indifference to people. " I am not at all of Mme du Deffand's opinion," he wrote to Crauford in 1766, " that one might as well be dead as not love somebody. I think one had better be dead than love anybody." He was undoubtedly more indifferent than is usual with sensitive and highly civilised persons. He may have trained himself (as he professed), to be so, on the principle " that it is impossible to love and to be wise," or he may have explained an indifference that was natural to him by saying that he desired and cultivated it. His curiosity in the many, his dutiful consideration

[1] Horace Walpole to Sir Horace Mann, May 4th, 1786.

for his family (even when, in the person of his mad nephew, his family could only be tiresome and exhausting), his love of books, pictures, curios, trinkets, dogs and cats, all these things served to drain from him any capacity for intense feeling about individuals. When Gray died in 1771 he wrote a curious letter to John Chute:

" As self lies so rooted in self, no doubt the nearness of our ages made the stroke recoil to my own breast; and having so little expected his death, it is plain how little I expect my own. Yet to you, who of all men living are the most forgiving, I need not excuse the concern I feel. I fear most men ought to apologise for their want of feeling, instead of palliating that sensation when they have it. I thought that what I had seen of the world had hardened my heart; but I find that it had formed my language, not extinguished my tenderness. In short, I am really shocked—nay, I am hurt at my own weakness, as I perceive that when I love anybody, it is for my life; and I have too much reason not to wish that such a disposition may very seldom be put to the trial. You, at least, are the only person to whom I would venture to make such a confession."[1]

Here is an extraordinary medley of ideas, put down with the clearness and correctness of expression which did not desert Walpole even when recording an emotional experience that he did not properly understand. Some styles keep the reader perpetually aware of the complexities inherent in thought and speech,

[1] Horace Walpole to John Chute, August 5th, 1771.

and, guiding him into curious ways, leave him stranded far from his destination. But Walpole's style is "a naked and open daylight"; his reader is never in danger of being benighted, and arrives by easy and comfortable stages at the writer's meaning. Nevertheless the writer's meaning may in itself be a curious compound. Here is Walpole making out that his distress for Gray's death was so acute that it must have been personal fear, but then suggesting that he says so only to avoid appearing weakly tender towards another person; he had in fact discovered that he was deceived in himself—he had not learnt indifference. Yet at the same time he reveals something not unlike pride in his emotion. "I fear," he says priggishly, "most men ought to apologise for their want of feeling, instead of palliating that sensation when they have it."

But although Walpole's genius for expression was equal to almost any strain which he might put upon it, undoubtedly the less important his matter the more his sense of artistry was stimulated. He never wrote a better letter than his apology to Lord Nuneham. No theme in the world has less intrinsic substance or interest than an apology for having mistaken the date of an engagement, but to Walpole any situation demanding the exercise of tact and *savoir faire* was interesting, and the more unimportant the issues were, the greater the opportunity it gave to his sophistication. As a great actor may be more famed for the way in which he says "Pray you undo this button" than for his delivery of "To be or not to be," so Walpole put as much of himself into a note of apology as into any of his famous descriptive letters—the visit to Ranelagh or the trial and execution of the rebel lords. It is characteristic that he exaggerates his distress, even to the point of foolishness in " I can never see my own face again "; he would never have passed the phrase if it had come from Mme du Deffand in a moment of ardour. Indeed one of the ways in which Walpole showed his distaste for excessive feeling was by using the language of emotion whenever a sufficiently trivial occasion arose.

" I am in such confusion, my dear Lord, that I do not know what to say, but the truth. I had read *Tuesday* on your Lordship's card instead of *Monday*, and never knew my mistake until this instant. My servant asked me what I would have for dinner! I replied, ' I dine at Lord Nuneham's.' He said ' I beg your pardon, Lord Nuneham's card was for yesterday; I thought your Honour had disengaged yourself.' I dined alone at home yesterday, and am shocked to think that I probably made your Lordship, Lady Nuneham, and your company wait. You will possibly forgive me, but I can never see my own face again—nor will ever read a card again without spectacles. Consider what pleasure I have lost, and pity

Your mortified humble servant,

HOR. WALPOLE."[1]

Walpole stands for the discretion and moderation of the eighteenth century. He was extravagant only

[1] Horace Walpole to Viscount Nuneham, May 1772.

in his hobbies and his compliments, and towards the end of his life we find him dismayed beyond measure by the French Revolution and out of sympathy with the riotous splendour of Devonshire House. He admired the Duchess Georgiana for her charms and graces, but had no illusions about her weaknesses. He said, when her first child was born, that she would stuff it into her knitting-bag and forget it whenever she wanted to play macao; and in telling the Berrys of the extravagances of the Duchess and her sister Lady Bessborough and of their enormous losses at cards he showed an obvious distaste. " Good Hannah More," who had just published her *Estimate of the Religion of the Fashionable World*, was far more to his liking. Horace Walpole and John Wesley, often mentioned together as chroniclers of the eighteenth century for the sake of the contrast between them, sometimes looked upon the world with very much the same eye.

A man need not appreciate all the tendencies and personalities of his age in order to take it in his grasp. Walpole's errors of judgment, his antipathies, his prejudices, the cruel letter he wrote to Chatterton but did not post, the reply to Cowper's friend Johnson which he did not even write, his refusal to allow Sir Joshua Reynolds to present Dr. Johnson to him at the Royal Academy—all these things contribute to the order to which he reduces for us the eighteenth century. The lack of intellectual integrity which distinguishes him so clearly from a man like Dr. Johnson, a certain absence of humanity which made him sneer at Johnson's self-imposed penances and his resolutions—" at near seventy *begins* to think of examining the proofs of that religion which he had believed so implicitly "—in some ways widened rather than narrowed Walpole's scope as a chronicler. (Mme du Deffand and Johnson would have understood one another, she at seventy asking Walpole whether he believed in a future life, apologising for her importunity, explaining that it was due to her fear of dying before seeing him again and her need to consult " un véritable ami avant de plier bagage.") Walpole's capacity for sympathy perhaps increased as he grew old, although even then it did not run either deep or strong. His devotion to Mary Berry and her sister gave him more concentrated anxiety than any earlier attachments, but it was partly the fearfulness that all timid elderly people feel as they see how ignorant and heedless of danger the young can be. To be fearful was also, for Walpole, part of the enchantment. While the temerity of the Miss Berrys travelling about Europe in the face of revolution horrified him, and the fear of losing such amiable companions prostrated him, no doubt he was fascinated by their nimbleness. It was incredible that anyone should be so indifferent to discomfort, so apt for movement over the globe.

Whether his infatuation for the Berrys endears Walpole to us, or makes him seem more foolish, unquestionably old age suited him. All his knowledge of kings and queens, lords and beauties, had lain in the cool cellars of his memory coming to its maturity. Physically, too, he was more fitted to be old than to be young. In youth and middle age his delicacy and timidity had often made him look ridiculous, in the seventies they became excusable; moreover, they had scarcely increased. Thanks to long care and self-restraint he could appear comparatively strong. In 1787, when he was driving down a dark lane from Mrs. Crewe's, his coach almost overturned and his teeth (which even in those days of primitive dentistry were all his own) came into sharp contact with the chaplain's skull. The coachman's underlip was much mangled, the coach had recourse to a coach-surgeon, but Walpole's teeth survived the shock to the interest and satisfaction of Richmond, Twickenham, Isleworth, and Hampton Court. "My teeth," he wrote, "have had cards and visits of howd' ye's." He excelled in fanciful humour about his bodily condition. Sea air and bathing might cure the Berrys, "on me they have no more effect than they would have on an Egyptian queen who has been embowelled and preserved in her sycamore *étui* ever since dying was first invented. . . . Mr. Huitson has teased me so much about jumbling my relics that I have aired them every morning in the coach for this fortnight; and yet you see I cannot write ten lines together!"[1] When Hannah More wrote to sympathise with him for his gout, he replied with a charming contentment:

"You commend me too for not complaining of my chronical evil; but, my dear Madam, I should be blameable for the reverse. If I would live to seventy-two, ought I not to compound for the encumbrances of old age? And who has fewer?

[1] Horace Walpole to Mary Berry, August 24th, 1796.

And who has more cause to be thankful to Providence for his lot? The gout, it is true, comes frequently, but the fits are short, and very tolerable; the intervals are full of health. My eyes are perfect, my hearing but little impaired, chiefly to whispers, for which I certainly have little occasion; my spirits never fail; and though my hands and feet are crippled, I can use both, and do not wish to box, wrestle, or dance a hornpipe. In short, I am just infirm enough to enjoy all the prerogatives of old age, and to plead them against anything that I have not a mind to do. Young men must conform to every folly in fashion: drink when they had rather be sober; fight a duel if somebody else is wrong-headed; marry to please their fathers, not themselves; and shiver in a white waistcoat, because ancient almanacs, copying the Arabian, placed the month of June after May; though, when the style was reformed, it ought to have been intercalated between December and January. Indeed, I have been so childish as to cut my hay for the same reason, and am now weeping over it by the fire-side."[1]

[1] Horace Walpole to Hannah More, July 2nd, 1789.

2. WALPOLE AND MME DU DEFFAND

Yet Mme du Deffand, twenty years earlier, had written to him:

". . . Je ne puis vous souhaiter de parvenir à une grande vieillesse; on ne peut être heureux qu'autant qu'on a l'esprit de son état, et celui d'un grand âge est d'être imbécile; on souffre trop quand on y conserve le sens commun."[1]

She was seventy-one at the time and had found nothing but horror in age, whether her own or others'. Weakness and vanity were all she could perceive left in her old friend Président Hénault. Walpole grew more content with life as he grew older. He was indeed a child of this world, amused and pleased to the end by people, books, animals, his "comfortable tea and bread and butter." The longer he lived, the more he learned to be satisfied with what was within his grasp. Mme du Deffand on the contrary came to the end of her life feeling that she had not known anyone or been known by anyone, and that she did not perhaps even know herself. She was unable to find any consolation for having been born, and nothing could fit her

[1] Mme du Deffand to Horace Walpole, March 21st, 1768.

for this life—and how did she know, if there were another life, that she would be more suited for it? Many differences can be traced between Walpole and Mme du Deffand, but this surely is the most fundamental—Walpole loved life and Mme du Deffand detested it. Many who begin by detesting it grow complacent in their old age, recognising the bonds between them and nature and their fellow beings, learning to ignore all that is out of joint; but so vital a spirit had Mme du Deffand that the years only deepened her estrangement. There she sat day after day for thirty years, blind in her *tonneau*, surrounded by people and voices, but in her spirit a perpetual nomad, searching for pasture in deserts that grew, it seemed, always vaster, emptier and more arid—not knowing why she was upon the earth, and yet unable to wish to leave it.

Mme du Deffand's early life is a little vague and general. She was the Regent's mistress for a fortnight, but so were others. She was a constant guest at Sceaux in its brilliant days, but other witty and charming women were also guests there, and her life, as far as we know, did not differ greatly from theirs. But when she becomes old and blind all vagueness passes from the picture. We can visualise her clearly, sitting in her arm-chair with its huge bonnet to shelter her small delicate person from draughts, in the rooms which had been Mme de Montespan's; the discreet, devoted Wiart, her secretary, in the background; in the foreground her stock companions, Président Hénault, falling to pieces with old age, Pont-de-Veyle in the corner of the chimney with his feet on the andirons; her visitors, the fairy creature, Mme de Choiseul, who, alas, turned out to be perfect, Selwyn either yawning or sleeping—but she preferred him to sleep. An old pensioner from the Invalides came at six or seven in the morning (really the middle of her night) and read to her for four hours as she lay in bed. Sometimes if he had not come she began dictating her letters to Walpole, or perhaps wrote a few lines in her own hand if it were too early to call for Wiart. Dr. Johnson's life is not more clear to us than the life of this old woman. Her little dog Tulipe (whose manners were bad) was in course of time replaced by Tonton (whose temper was shocking) but otherwise the *tableau vivant* scarcely changed for twenty years, and by simple persistence deserved and won its immortality. Mme du Deffand's only hobby was the unravelling of pieces of material, a curious symbol of her delicately destructive nature; the unravelled strands were afterwards rewoven into cloth and given to her friends. She circumvented her blindness so well that even in her presence it was difficult to realise it; her talk and her letters were those of a person in full possession of all her faculties. It is possible that Walpole writing with " une férocité sarmate " forgot that no letter Mme du Deffand ever received could be private, that his most insulting words could not remain in the silence in which he wrote them but must be read aloud if they were ever to perform the final stage of their journey from his mind to hers.

It was only a year after her rupture with Mlle de

Lespinasse that Horace Walpole visited Paris and obtained an introduction to Mme du Deffand. In January 1766 he wrote a long letter to Gray on the French character, describing in detail several notable persons, Mme du Deffand among them.

"Madame du Deffand . . . is now very old and stone blind, but retains all her vivacity, wit, memory, judgment, passions, and agreeableness. She goes to operas, plays, suppers, and Versailles; gives suppers twice a week; has everything new read to her; makes new songs and epigrams, ay, admirably, and remembers every one that has been made these fourscore years. She corresponds with Voltaire, dictates charming letters to him, contradicts him, is no bigot to him or anybody, and laughs both at the clergy and the philosophers. In a dispute, into which she easily falls, she is very warm, and yet scarce ever in the wrong; her judgment on every subject is as just as possible; for she is all love and hatred, passionate for her friends to enthusiasm, still anxious to be loved, I don't mean by lovers, and a vehement enemy, but openly. As she can have no amusement but conversation, the least solitude and *ennui* are insupportable to her, and put her into the power of several worthless people, who eat her suppers when they can eat nobody's of higher rank; wink to one another and laugh at her; hate her because she has forty times more parts—and venture to hate her because she is not rich."[1]

Let us note the parenthesis "I don't mean by lovers." From this time it became one of the chief

[1] Horace Walpole to Thomas Gray, January 25th, 1766.

dreads of Walpole's life that anyone should imagine that the intimacy between him and Mme du Deffand was anything more than friendship. The very circumstances which made such a thing improbable even as a rumour—her age and her blindness—constituted the chief grounds for his embarrassment. Like many vain and clever people, Walpole developed to perfection the trick of forestalling mockery by his own witty exaggerations of his weaknesses. He called himself a *pantin* and said that he had the temperament of a gentleman usher. But the vain, even when clever enough to protect themselves in this way, may have spots too tender for the compassionate investigation of their own fingers. For Walpole such a spot had been created by his relationship with Mme du Deffand. Even with regard to a man friend such as Gray, and when writing to another friend as close as Chute, Walpole could be morbid and self-conscious. Before the advent of the Berrys he usually addressed his women friends in a tone of inflated gallantry, and between this gallantry and his insolence to Mme du Deffand lies a close connection. Until almost the end of his life he did not know how to treat women simply and normally; he was in this the opposite of the bourgeois Cowper with his exquisite tact and delicacy. For no less than fourteen years Walpole lived in terror of waking up one day to find that the latest laughing-stock in the world of fashion was Horace Walpole, a bachelor of over fifty who had taken a blind French mistress twenty years his senior. It did not reassure him to be told by Mme du Deffand that in France no one would believe any man to be the lover of a woman of seventy unless they knew that he was paid for it. Oddly enough in 1753 he had written an essay for *The World*, a fashionable weekly then newly started by Edward Moore, in which he advocated " the sensual pleasure of Love " as the " great cordial of life " and old women as the proper objects of that love. " I might enumerate a thousand reasons . . . as the fickleness of youth, the caprices of beauty and its transient state, the jealousy from rivals, the distraction from having children. . . ." And—so he went on—it is natural as well as advisable for men to love old women, " for unless there was implanted in our natures a strong temptation towards the love of elderly women, why should the very first prohibition in the table of consanguinity forbid a man to marry his grandmother? " Then he gave a list of old women who had inspired love—Sarah, Helen of Troy, Queen Elizabeth, Diane de Poitiers and Ninon de Lenclos—saying of the last " How unfortunate am I, that she did not live a few years longer, that I might have had the opportunity of wearing her chains." (It was she who had the Marquis de Sévigné, both father and son, among her lovers.) At the time of publication this essay caused a stir and the authorship probably did not long remain a secret. Walpole was quite vain enough to suppose it had not been forgotten in 1766 and to be plagued by the thought that in his friendship with Mme du Deffand, gossip would credit him with practising in sincerity what he had preached in levity. His fear of ridicule was abnormal even for those days of poisoned arrows. Mme du Deffand at the end of a life spent in quizzing human nature declared that she had never met a weakness to resemble it. When years later his feeling for Miss Mary Berry was so strong that he could not read a letter from her " temperately " until he had first searched through it for some mention of her stomach-ache, he assured Lady Ossory that he did not care a straw if people said he was in love with one of the sisters. He was too old to bother about " the *qu'en dit-on* " and the ridicule could fall only on him, not on them.[1] It did not occur to him that (unless there is some curious ordinance by which a young man is ridiculous when loved by an old woman, but a young woman is not ridiculous when loved by an old man) the ridicule could fall only on Mme du Deffand, not on him. In any case he was terrified. He imposed strictures upon her conversation and on her manner of addressing him, and his tone in writing to her seems to have been constantly peevish and carping, and not seldom abusive. He himself admitted to Lady Hervey in 1766 that he had " scolded Madame du Deffand black and blue." And so we may judge from her replies he continued to do while she lived. Eleven of his letters to her exist in recently discovered copies made by the French Secret Service when the originals were in the post. Seven others were accidentally saved among Mme du Deffand's papers, and the total written cannot have been far short of eight hundred. Walpole was very careful to get from Mme du Deffand at intervals any letters of his that she did not burn, and he gave

[1] Horace Walpole to the Countess of Upper Ossory, May 29th, 1792.

instructions about them to Miss Berry which apparently she fulfilled after his death. Some passages (probably marked by him for the purpose) were published in footnotes in Miss Berry's edition of Mme du Deffand's letters, but the letters themselves were almost certainly burned. Walpole told his cousin Conway, as a reason for troubling him to carry back some of the letters from France, that he was ashamed of his poor French.

There are no grounds for supposing that Mme du Deffand entertained for a moment the thought that Walpole might be her lover, or ever wished for such a thing, but quite clearly she was ardently in love with him. She speaks of the possibility of not seeing him again as a loss to which she must resign herself as she did to the loss of her eyes. Her language cannot be misunderstood, she felt a miracle in her breast, all the more beautiful and astounding because her life had always been solitary and unsatisfying. "Vous me rendrez dévote," cried the old woman whose scepticism at fifteen had baffled Massillon, "vous me ferez reconnaître une Providence, vous réparerez toutes les injustices que j'ai éprouvées, vous dissiperez tous mes chagrins, tous mes ennuis, je ne craindrai plus mes ennemis, leurs armes deviendront des épingles, nous nous moquerons des faux dieux, nous renverserons peut-être leurs autels."[1] The ecstasy and confidence are those of love but the theme that of King Lear going with Cordelia to prison, to pray and sing and tell old tales and laugh at gilded butterflies:

[1] Mme du Deffand to Horace Walpole, May 5th, 1766.

" And take upon's the mystery of things,
As if we were God's spies."

On the narrow ultimate ledge to which her years and blindness had driven her Mme du Deffand found life at last endowed with meaning and value through the supposed affection and understanding of Horace Walpole.

But she made a horrible mistake, and we who have eighteen volumes of Walpole's letters and know him far better than she ever did, blush for it. He was not a person to whom one could speak as King Lear spoke to Cordelia, to whom one could fittingly cry " Vous me rendrez dévote, vous me ferez reconnaître une Providence, vous réparerez toutes les injustices que j'ai éprouvées. . . ." The direction of Mme du Deffand's mind and the quality of her emotions made her so different from Walpole, that we feel an impropriety in her opening her heart to him, a sense of something holy given to the dogs. Yet there was nothing base about Walpole, he was not by any means without capacity for feeling, but the tenor of his inner life differed so much from that of his friend that between them there could be no becoming or profitable intimacy. Mme du Deffand, in spite of her elegance, her " bon ton," her scepticism, took a view of life Calvinistic in its seriousness. " Quelle cruauté de se marier, tirer des individus du néant," she exclaims in a letter to Walpole, and one feels that he read it with about as much comprehension as he would a novel by Dostoevsky. In all their social, and many of their literary interests, they had complete sympathy. But when Mme du Deffand—in correspondence—tried to carry the sympathy beyond the social and the literary, disclosing the private intensity of her existence and soliciting similar disclosures from Walpole, she only emphasised the difference between them. Walpole shrank to a veritable puppet, designing Gothic wall-paper and walking like a dabchick. Mme du Deffand grew to the dignity of a heroine in Racine, to a personality with sorrows too deep to be individual —noble and moving in herself, but considered in her relation to the adored *pantin*, almost grotesque. Walpole understood the situation better than Mme du Deffand. The non-tragic character is wiser in his generation than the tragic. Mme du Deffand fought with Walpole as though she was struggling with a spirit of her own quality, and his lack of response or his downright cruelty she put down to reasons which would have been relevant in her emotional world, but were for him so irrelevant that he felt them indecent.

Owing to the destruction or disappearance of the bulk of his letters to her there remains only one critical occasion on which we can see Walpole's methods at first hand. In the Spring of 1773 the permanent dispute had risen to one of its many climaxes, and two of Walpole's letters written at this time were amongst those copied by the French Secret Service. In February we find Mme du Deffand on the verge of exasperation, crying "Au nom de Dieu, soyez tranquille!" Then in March follow from her two very stiff brief notes; on March 31st, however, she begins to unbend, explaining that she had been deeply hurt by his letter early in the month in which he had said, to quote her italicised words, " *que vous étiez excédé de mes lettres, que vous les haïssiez à la mort, que vous aimeriez mieux être une connaissance que mon ami.*" But meanwhile on March 30th Walpole in London had written in reply to her cold note of March 10th:

" Je n'ai plus rien à dire, Madame, je vois l'impossibilité qu'il y a d'accorder deux humeurs aussi opposées que la vôtre et la mienne, et je ne ferai plus d'efforts pour rendre agréable un commerce dont à force de me tourmenter vous m'avez entièrement dégoûté: qu'il aille tout au hasard.

" Si vous me faites l'honneur de m'écrire des lettres auxquelles on peut répondre, j'y répondrai. Sinon vous me dispenserez, je crois, d'écrire, car je ne vois pas la nécessité d'une correspondance régulière, quand on est si peu content l'un de l'autre."

We have no reply from Mme du Deffand to this, nor any letters from her for three weeks. Any she wrote were probably destroyed by Walpole, as Mrs. Toynbee has suggested. The next letter is one from Walpole.

" Londres, 13 avril, 1773.

" Après beaucoups de dégoûts on ne revient pas facilement à la bonne humeur, je vous avoue que je m'attendrai toujours à des persécutions nouvelles, et cette crainte m'ôte tout le plaisir du commerce. J'écris sans envie d'écrire, et je reçois des lettres sans envie de les ouvrir; plus les querelles se réitèrent, plus les raccommodements sont difficiles, et à la fin deviennent impossibles. Je regarde cette conclusion de notre liaison comme immanquable et de là je deviens tous les jours moins soigneux à l'éviter. . . ."

Considering that Walpole was not writing in his own language, we must admire the lucidity of his expression, if we can admire nothing else. One is not surprised that the loyal Miss Berry left no traces of these documents. The quotations which she makes are special morsels, no scoldings that are not temperate and dignified, passages of advice worthy of a Christian and a Stoic. Mme du Deffand has written saying that she has abandoned any idea of arriving at happiness, for too many conditions are necessary, so she will just yawn in her *tonneau* and refuse to be perturbed by what goes on around it.[1] Walpole (quoted by Miss Berry) replies with gentle mockery—Walpole who was so seldom unhappy—asking how she could still be so childish as to think of happiness, the prerogative only of idiots. Then with typical lack of logic he insists that both of them are a thousand times happier than beggars, prisoners or the sick, and not much less happy than princes and people of fortune. " Voilà une réflexion qui me donne de la véritable dévotion. Je rends grâce à la Providence de mon sort, et je n'envie personne."[2]

The only excuse for Walpole is that he was talking in unfamiliar terms to a person whose feelings he could not appreciate and whose attachment was not

[1] Mme du Deffand to Horace Walpole, June 13th, 1770.
[2] Horace Walpole to Mme du Deffand, June 20th, 1770.

only ludicrous from a superficial and social point of view, but (since he was the object of the attachment) basically incongruous. His constant harshness brought about a condition of morbid sensibility in Mme du Deffand; it was only too easy to find quarrel in a straw; she lost her sense of humour and thought when he threatened playfully not to write for a week that he did it in irritation because she had begged for news of his health. Early in their friendship she told him that she had lost her confidence for ever; but she misjudged her own powers of recuperation; confidence returned again and again. One month she might be utterly crushed and hopeless, the next found her turning the brightness of her wit on to their duel. "Soyons *amis* (si ce mot n'est pas malsonnant), mais amis sans amitié; c'est un système nouveau, mais dans le fond pas plus incompréhensible que la Trinité."[1] At another time she was prepared to admit that she had overreached herself, that Walpole was not worth all that she felt for him. But even so there was no cure for it and the fault lay with neither of them; it was for her to spare him reproaches, for him to spare her reprimands. And whatever she might see or admit nothing altered her conviction that there remained no pleasure in life except to pour out one's heart to a friend. But Walpole did not agree; it was not for the pleasure of "épanchement" that he corresponded with Sir Horace Mann for forty years. Out of his element, discomposed, seeking for a means to regain his composure, he was sometimes brutal and sometimes merely

[1] Mme du Deffand to Horace Walpole, October 19th, 1766.

foolish. " Je suis refroidi " he wrote, thinking he had found a secret for bringing the relationship to a temperature more suitable to his nature.

On the other hand, as has often been noted in Walpole's favour, he returned to Paris four times in nine years in order to see Mme du Deffand, enduring eight times over a journey almost as difficult and uncomfortable as that from London to Iceland to-day. Self-love is not the entire explanation of Walpole's character, and love is not by any means the entire explanation of Mme du Deffand's. Walpole, as friends go, was both conscientious and generous. Sir Horace Mann, who coveted the Order of the Bath and two small black spaniels for the Duchess of Tuscany, never seems to have wearied Walpole by his fussy importunity. He offered to share his not unlimited wealth at one time with Conway and at another with Mme du Deffand, making the offer in both cases with supreme delicacy. " Je voudrais," he wrote to Mme du Deffand, " que la somme ne me fût pas aussi indifférente qu'elle l'est."[1] But to Walpole love and friendship were two perfectly distinct things. He was capable of reciprocating friendship, but not love, and nothing is so apt to make love appear improper as absence of reciprocation.

Yet he admired Mme du Deffand, even calling her his charming old passion, and was profoundly flattered to be idolised by her. Her adoption of the attitude of a pupil was peculiarly gratifying to a man who dared not indulge in public a tendency towards pedagogy. One

[1] Horace Walpole to Mme du Deffand, February 9th, 1770.

sometimes wonders if this was not one of the threads upon which Mme du Deffand consciously held him. " De plus," she said, " on est sensible à être aimé, ne fut-ce que de la Tulipe,"[1] Tulipe the predecessor of Tonton, the dog Walpole inherited when Mme du Deffand died. Moreover he was fully awake to her remarkable gifts. He wished for a portrait of Mme de Maintenon to place opposite that of Mme du Deffand —the first he would call the artificial, and the second, the natural. Even Mme de Sévigné's letters had no right to discourage her about her own, he assured her; she ought to be content with them—" je le suis infiniment." He could not scold every week, and sometimes her arguments and assurances calmed him; but there was no knowing when or upon what pretext he would not start reviling her again. " Depuis feu Protée," she jibed, " personne n'a été si dissemblable d'un jour à l'autre que vous l'êtes."[2] Mme du Deffand was not the sort of woman who could for ever turn the other cheek even if her assailant were the man she loved. Her letters at times must have sunk deep into the tenderest parts of Walpole's vanity. Even on her death-bed she did not spare him. When she criticised the phrase " homme de condition " in a letter he had written to Voltaire, it was wounding enough to say that the words would appear " une vanité " without adding " et peut-être il dira qu'il ne savait pas que les gens de condition eussent des privilèges différents des autres quand ils se font auteurs."[3] Poor Walpole, one must

[1] Mme du Deffand to Horace Walpole, April 24th, 1766.
[2] *Ditto*, March 21st, 1768. [3] *Ditto*, June 28th, 1768.

remember, had conquered a woman of a bitter, proud and penetrating mind. Those who capture a dragon may find chains of little value when the creature breathes flame.

But when they met, all difficulties melted; she forgot his brutalities and he forgot her indiscretions. With her genius for conversation and her blind sensitiveness to the mood of her companion, Mme du Deffand in the flesh would never embarrass Walpole as Mme du Deffand in her letters so often did. And Walpole, realising in her presence how frail and old she really was, no doubt treated her with every courtesy. But the contest went on until the very end of her life. In a letter to Walpole, written a few weeks before her death, she said " Je n'ouvre pas une de vos lettres que je n'y trouve quelques réprimandes. La dernière a été longue et peu méritée."[1] In the last letter of all, knowing that she was dying, she wrote "Divertissez-vous, mon ami, le plus que vous pourrez; ne vous affligez point de mon état; nous étions presque perdus l'un pour l'autre; nous ne nous devions jamais revoir; vous me regretterez, parce qu'on est bien aise de se savoir aimé."[2] Wiart—to her surprise—wept as he wrote the words; the shallowest and most indifferent of friends could scarcely have read them without distress, and Walpole was genuinely moved. He wrote at once to his cousin Thomas Wal-

[1] Mme du Deffand to Horace Walpole, August 3rd, 1780.

[2] *Ditto*, August 22nd, 1780. Note the similarity to the phrase quoted on p. 63, from the fourth letter she ever wrote to him. This letter of August 22nd, 1780, is numbered 838 in Mrs. Paget Toynbee's complete edition of Mme du Deffand's correspondence with Walpole.

pole in Paris: "My dear old friend's last letter shocked me as much as possible. . . . I entreat you to tell her—but I do not know how to express how much I love her and how much I feel."[1] But by the time that the letter arrived her state was so precarious that the attendants did not dare to read her his message. The bitterness and sadness of her last words had carried him out of his world into hers, and so he stammered, just too late for her to hear, something about feeling and love. But it was only for a moment; a little further on in the same letter he says: "I can scarcely bear to name it, but should the worst happen, I beg, my dear Sir, that you will get from M. Wiart all my letters, and keep them till you come."

[1] Horace Walpole to Thomas Walpole, September 6th, 1780.

3. MME DU DEFFAND

There is nothing completely new in any period of literature or civilisation. Many men before Keats had wished for a life of sensations rather than of thoughts. The classicism of Jane Austen was not out of place in the world of Blake, Scott, Wordsworth and Coleridge, and when Mme du Deffand insisted that the life of feeling was the only reality, there were people alive in the world who could understand her and agree with her, although Walpole was not among them. In her relation to Horace Walpole, and in her submission to the heart's need to find an object for its affections, Mme du Deffand belongs to the artists and writers of the Romantic Revival. She is not the less true to the eighteenth century, which bred many romantics, but the age which sympathised fully with her philosophy was coming into being only as she died—and that through the activities of her enemies the Encyclopædists, through the influence of the " knave and fool " (as she called him) Rousseau.

The causes of the antipathy between Mme du Deffand and the Encyclopædists were various. The absence of style and harmony in Rousseau outraged her. " C'est un sophiste, un esprit faux et forcé; son esprit est un instrument discord, il en joue avec beaucoup d' exécution, mais il déchire les oreilles de ceux qui en ont."[1] " No doubt," says Lytton Strachey in his essay upon Mme du Deffand, " her dislike of the Encyclopædists and all their works was in part a matter of personal pique—the result of her famous quarrel with Mademoiselle de Lespinasse, under whose opposing banner d'Alembert and all the intellectual leaders of Parisian society had unhesitatingly ranged themselves."[2] Walpole told her that she measured friendship, truth, wit, everything according to the homage rendered to her. He exaggerated, for she was not prone to credit even those who paid her homage with particular virtues or talents, but there was nevertheless some ground for his accusation.

For Walpole's dislike of the Encyclopædists one need not look so far. He made fun of them readily with Mme du Deffand, or with anyone, because he was not an intellectually minded person. He never enquired into causes nor wished to master knowledge. While his mind was an excellent one for the mere incidents of contemporary life, a philosophy of history would have been altogether outside its range. Moreover he suffered from the self-imposed impotence of the snob; he would have been ashamed to devote himself to any cause that might involve him in even temporary neglect of social distinctions. This disability Mme du Deffand did not share with him, for

[1] Mme du Deffand to Horace Walpole, March 9th, 1777.
[2] *Books and Characters*, by Lytton Strachey.

she was no snob, although her sense of class division was acute. While Mme de Sévigné regarded the peasantry with cruelty in general, but with kindness in particular, it seems rarely to have entered Mme du Deffand's head that the lower classes existed.

Different as the forms of their egoism were, yet egoism lay at the bottom of the lack of sympathy which both Mme du Deffand and Walpole showed for the intellectual movements of their times. Scientific and historical matters interested Mme du Deffand as little as social problems. Foreign lands, excepting England, meant nothing to her; the past (earlier than Louis XIV) was negligible and the future incredible. Yet her egoism had none of the pettiness of Walpole's. She did not want any of the smaller comforts and satisfactions of life; she did not want fame or flattery and she took no satisfaction in either possessions or aristocratic connections. She craved only for the supreme interest of love to deliver her from friendships hollow and outworn and from the brittle and insecure consolations of a *salon*. Walpole's egoism dissipated itself in trifles. He was furiously acquisitive. "Two porters have just brought home my purchases from Mrs. Kennon the mid-wife's sale: Brobdingnag combs, old broken pots, pans, and pipkins, a lantern of scraped oyster-shells, scimitars, Turkish pipes, Chinese baskets, etc., etc."[1] This was in 1756; nearly thirty years later he confessed to Mason that he had always loved what money would purchase. "The

[1] Horace Walpole to the Hon. Henry Seymour Conway, February 12th, 1756.

whole of my philosophy consists in reconciling myself to buying fewer baubles for a year or two that I may live, and when the old child's baby-house is quite full of playthings."[1] Personality, no doubt, broadens and extends itself by possession, and we may foreshadow our ultimate absorption in the universe by gathering about us inanimate objects which are significant and beautiful. But the process is meaningless without selection; at times Walpole seems to have considered acquisition a virtue in itself, and at such moments he was ready to take a junk-shop to his bosom. One of the most illuminating of his disputes with Mme du Deffand occurred over Montaigne. Walpole read the essays at Bath, and complained that they bored him even more than Bath. He called Montaigne pedantry in its second childhood, a rhapsody of disconnected commonplaces. He scoffed at the idea of learning how to die—" la chose du monde qu'on est le plus sûr de faire sans l'avoir apprise "—and accused Montaigne of vanity, egotism, contradictions and uselessness.[2] Mme du Deffand parried easily; she was perfectly unconvinced. Montaigne was the only good philosopher and metaphysician there had ever been, and she could not understand Walpole's objection to " Le *je* et le *moi*," for what knowledge had we that did not originate in " le je et le moi "?[3] She suggested that if Walpole examined himself he would find resemblances in this and other respects between himself and Mon-

[1] Horace Walpole to the Rev. William Mason, February 2nd, 1784.
[2] Horace Walpole to Mme du Deffand, October 10th, 1766.
[3] Mme du Deffand to Horace Walpole, October 27th, 1766.

taigne. There she went astray, for a profound difference exists between the " I " and the " me " of Walpole and the " I " and " me " of Montaigne and Mme du Deffand. Walpole's self who figures (as Mme du Deffand suggested) very frequently and freely in his letters, is histrionic by comparison with the selves of Montaigne and Mme du Deffand. It is Walpole's idea of himself subtly modified by what he knows or suspects to be the idea of all who admire him and of his correspondent of the moment. A great deal had to be held back as not suitable for presentation. Revelation of the entire self, as it appears to itself in the silence and isolation of the night—Mme du Deffand's " I "—shocked and alarmed him. He was afraid of what he might find in himself if he examined too closely, and the very act of revelation offended his sense of good taste. To call Walpole a philosopher, as Mme du Deffand did, was rank nonsense; since the first principle of philosophy is to be afraid of nothing except missing the truth.

It was inevitable that Mme du Deffand's confidences were often very little to Walpole's taste, and that she on the other hand was not always in the humour to collect the tittle-tattle which he valued even more than the chattels of a midwife. But whether she was in the humour or not, she did not dare to default, knowing it to be the chief bond in their commerce. When she heard a piece of news or scandal likely to entertain him she displayed it in the retelling with the ingenuity and artistry of a merchant who cannot afford to let the smallest of his jewels be overlooked or undervalued. But the difference between her attitude and Walpole's to the same events often comes out clearly in their comments.

" . . . Tout cela vous aurait bien diverti si vous aviez été ici; mais vraiment il y a une autre histoire qui fait bien tomber la nôtre: c'est celle de M. de Thiard et de Mme de Monaco. Il y a trois semaines qu'elle est arrivée, et il n'y a que quatre jours qu' on la sait: ces deux personnes étant allées souper chez Mme de Beuvron, ne voulurent point se mettre à table, et au lieu de rester dans la chambre ou dans le cabinet, elles allèrent dans un petit boudoir tout au bout de l'appartement. Après le souper, Mme de Monaco aborda Mme de Beuvron avec l'air tout troublé et tout déconcerté; elle lui dit qu'il lui était arrivé le plus grand malheur du monde. 'Ah! vous avez cassé mes porcelaines? il n'y a pas grand mal.'—'Non, Madame, cela est bien pis.'—'Vous avez donc gâté mon ottomane?'—'Ah! mon Dieu non, cela est encore bien pis!'—'Mais qu'est-ce donc qui est arrivé? qu'avez-vous pu faire?'—'J'ai vu un très-joli secrétaire, nous avons eu la curiosité de voir comme il était en dedans; nous avons essayé nos clefs pour tâcher de l'ouvrir; il s'en est caché une dans la serrure.'—'Ah! Madame, cela est-il possible? il faut que vous le disiez vous-même pour que cela puisse se croire.'—Un valet de chambre que l'on soupçonnait d'avoir vu cette opération, fut sollicité par prières et promesses d'aller chercher un serrurier pour raccommoder la serrure; il n'en voulut rien faire, et dit qu'il se garderait bien de toucher à ce qui appartenait à sa maîtresse: la crainte, ou plûtôt la certitude d'être dénoncée par cet homme, détermina à le prévenir, en en faisant l'aveu. Voudriez-vous être à la place de M. Thiard? Pour moi, j' aimerais mieux avoir été surprise en mettant la main dans la poche; il y aurait du moins de l'adresse et moins de perfidie; cela est horrible. . . ."[1]

Walpole characteristically, was either not very shocked or would not appear so. Lord Hertford (his cousin) he said would hang himself if he knew it, being an ardent admirer of the Princesse de Monaco. "Mais réellement," expostulated Walpole, "le cavalier était bien maladroit d'employer si lourdement son temps dans un boudoir avec la plus jolie femme de France, et une femme un peu disposée à la curiosité. Mon dévot cousin s'y serait pris d'une autre façon."[2] But the ultimate significance of an act could not escape Mme du Deffand's attention, however good the comedy of the act itself. "Perfidie," she said, "cela est horrible." Walpole could overlook her moralising for the sake of her tale, but what he could not tolerate was her standing between him and the people she was describing, clouding the whole scene with her own boredom, or in her dissatisfaction stripping the figures of her friends until they scarcely possessed the colour or shape of living things. Mme du Deffand understood far too much; her distinctions were too wide; she was not content to classify her acquaintances as clever, stupid, pretty, ugly, old, young, cold, passionate. "Mon Dieu, mon Dieu, quelle différence il y a d'une

[1] Mme du Deffand to Horace Walpole, June 3rd, 1766.
[2] Horace Walpole to Mme du Deffand, June 1766.

âme à une autre! J'y en trouve une aussi grande que d'un ange à une huître."[1] And yet while this is the current of her feeling a cross-current breaks in from time to time, pleating the surface of her likes and dislikes in fascinating and complicated designs—the cross-current of the snobbishness of a drawing-room, a *petit cercle* surrounded by real or imaginary enemies—Verdurinism. For Mme du Deffand's delight in the charms of Mme de Choiseul is not unlike the delight of Mme Verdurin in Odette de Creçy.[2] Mme du Deffand goes to sup with the Choiseuls. M. de Thiers is there, M. de Castellane, and the Abbé Barthélemy.

" Quand j'arrivai on vint au-devant de moi en me criant, ' Point de circonspection, point de circonspection, et surtout point de circonspection! ' Je le promis, et je tins fidèlement parole. Le premier début fut que l'époux dit qu'on l'avait voulu retenir à souper chez Mme de Beauvau; je lui demandai qu'est-ce qui y soupait. Quand il eut tout nommé, ' Vous ne devez pas y avoir regret,' lui dis-je, ' et tout ce que nous sommes ici, nous valons mieux, pièce pour pièce.' Ce ' pièce pour pièce ' réussit infiniment, et plut beaucoup à la grand'maman.[3] L'après souper fut encore plus gai, et après le départ du Castellane la confiance fut encore plus grande."[4]

[1] Sometimes—not unnaturally—she held the opposite view, that everyone was alike (see her letter of May 31st, 1768). But both views were equally distant from Walpole's attitude.

[2] See *Du Côté de Chez Swann*, by Marcel Proust.

[3] Nickname for the Duchesse de Choiseul.

[4] Mme du Deffand to Horace Walpole, March 17th, 1767.

One cannot avoid the comparison—there is the same over-valuation of any joke made by a member of the *petit cercle*, especially a joke at the expense of any person outside it, the same suspicion of any person that may not be entirely in sympathy—" après le départ du Castellane la confiance fut encore plus grande."

Again when Mme du Deffand quarrelled with anyone she had admitted to intimacy with her, the rupture was of mortal severity. The former friend became not merely an enemy but a traitor. Mme de Rochefort, whom she had loved passionately, was " infidèle "; no more was said. Mlle de Lespinasse had been a daughter to her for ten years, but an hour sufficed to cut her out of her life and her affections for ever. Twelve years after she wrote to Walpole:

" Mlle de Lespinasse est morte cette nuit, à deux heures après minuit; ç'aurait été pour moi autrefois un évènement, aujourd'hui ce n'est rien de tout."[1]

It is not surprising that many of the comments of such a woman should be two-edged, that she frequently spared her friends only a little less than her enemies. Against the character of Mme de Forcalquier she had nothing at all, it was certainly a very good character—" mais elle n'a attrapé qu'une étincelle du flambeau de Prométhée." Selwyn being a friend of Walpole's, she was kindly disposed towards him and remarked that he was the best creature in the world, faithful as a little dog, never boring—" on ne peut

[1] Mme du Deffand to Horace Walpole, May 22nd, 1776.

guère avoir de conversation avec lui, mais on n'est cependant point embarrassée du tête-à-tête." Even Mme de Sévigné, dead and a genius, she did not spare. "Oh! je ne ressemble point à Mme de Sévigné, vous avez raison, je suis à cent milles lieues de son esprit et de sa grâce" (the fingers pause a moment, unravelling the silk, and then without pity, move on) "et de l'intérêt qu'elle prenait à tout ce qui ne lui faisait rien."[1]

She makes the same criticism over and over again—people are busy about nothing; they move, they speak, they laugh; but it has no significance. They are automatons, Robots. And even if it were not so, her taste for living has gone, "nothingness" has taken the place of the natural appetites and interests—only the power to love intensely a single person remains and that has brought her more unhappiness than happiness. She often returns to this "nothingness." "Je ne trouve en moi que le néant, et il est aussi mauvais de trouver le néant en soi, qu'il serait heureux d'être resté dans le néant."[2] Her mind was always turning things about, looking upon the underside of commonplaces. She did not think one would be happier if one had the opportunity of a second life on earth with the experience gained in the first; since one would know people better, it would be the more distasteful to need them—"*et quand on n'est pas heureux est-on sage?*" She held a desolating view of the spirit which dominates society. "Il n'y a pas une seule personne à qui on puisse confier ses peines, sans lui donner une maligne joie et sans

[1] Mme du Deffand to Horace Walpole, March 21st, 1767.
[2] *Ditto*, June 26th, 1768.

s'avilir à ses yeux."[1] One called those friends, she said, by whom one was not afraid of being assassinated.

All this irritated Walpole. He told her she expected too much of her acquaintances, too much attention to her own tastes and emotions. He advised her how to regulate her life in order to avoid boredom. Had he been altogether the man of the world he posed as, he might have ridiculed her impatience and dissatisfaction. But he had at times felt a misanthropy not so remote from hers, when he confessed his disgust for the mountains of roast beef " roughly hewn out into the outlines of human form " whom he met at Houghton, men revealed as cannibals when they brandished their knives to carve a roast. The very fact that she irritated him suggests the existence of a sensitive cord which both were holding, and there are aspects from which they seem complements of one another, Mme du Deffand romantic by disposition, classic by taste and training, Walpole classic by disposition but romantic by taste and training. In a letter written in 1767 Mme du Deffand framed her superb expostulation against reason—particularly superb coming from one who had lived in the age of reason and (as she said to Walpole) always been the sworn enemy of everything and everyone possessing the least trace of romantic excess. (Yet she confessed that what she admired most in Mme de Sévigné's letters was her tenderness to her daughter.)

" Ah! la raison, la raison! Qu'est-ce que c'est que la raison? quel pouvoir a-t-elle? quand est-ce qu'elle

[1] Mme du Deffand to Horace Walpole, April 18th, 1769.

parle? quand est-ce qu'on peut l'écouter? quel bien procure-t-elle? Elle triomphe des passions? cela n'est pas vrai; et si elle arrêtait les mouvements de notre âme, elle serait cent fois plus contraire à notre bonheur que les passions ne peuvent l'être; ce serait vivre pour sentir le néant, et le néant (dont je fais grand cas) n'est bon que parce qu'on ne le sent pas."[1]

It is one of the oddest things in the history of human relationship, this grimly honest old woman—" une vieille sibylle retirée dans le coin d'un couvent "—filled to the brim with disillusion, without a shred of religion from her girlhood, pouring out her deepest thoughts and feelings to Horace Walpole, turning to him for counsel, listening to his facile orthodoxy, his commonplace assurances that life was good and death did not mean the end. It is hardly credible that she accepted his grounds for belief in a future life, and yet was aghast at his admiration for Crébillon, and gave as her reason for admiring Montaigne that he destroyed " la présomption du savoir." But perhaps there are no critical faculties so sharp that fear of death will not blunt them, and for all Mme du Deffand's independence, she suffered from the diffidence of a person knowing herself more loving than loved. Deliberately she had spent herself in a losing battle against time and indifference, and she faced death with both courage and energy exhausted. If we compare her letters with those of Dorothy Osborne or Mrs. Carlyle, hers seem lacking in resilience. There is little humour in them and no tranquillity. But where else in all letter-

[1] Mme du Deffand to Horace Walpole, May 23rd, 1767.

writing do we find age, intelligence and the deepest emotions so strangely combined? In these letters of Mme du Deffand a lifetime of experience, years of intellectual refinement and a most mature and lucid style are all put to the service of an emotion which normally burns itself out before either experience or intellect or style has grown equal to its perplexities. And so sensitive is the tissue of her writing that by her letters we seem to read the destroyed correspondence of Walpole. The marks of his words are on her replies like the bruises on delicate flesh and it is hard to believe when we have read her eight hundred letters that we have not read his too.

4. MÉRIMÉE

A little less than a century after Horace Walpole's birth there was born in Paris a letter-writer who proved to be almost as profuse and talented as Walpole himself. Another lonely, rather coddled child grew into another young man of acutely developed sociability, who became quickly a man of the world, addicted to politics, a dilettante interested in relics of the past, and yet remained all his life delicate and effeminate—in his last years, an elderly bachelor of " flimsy texture," spared gout only to be afflicted by lumbago, taking a mischievous pleasure in describing his frailty: " Je suis arrivé ici il y a quelques jours en assez bon état de conservation "—more often " en assez mauvais état." This was Prosper Mérimée, but his resemblances to Walpole go only far enough to justify our placing them in a pair of sconces—the quality of the wax and the flame is altogether different. Even their childhoods were essentially unlike. While Walpole at Eton refashioned his day-dreams, as he passed from Theocritus to Virgil or from Virgil to Mme de Scudéry, in the atmosphere of ease and security natural to a young English aristocrat in the reign of George II, Mérimée, born of superior bourgeois stock, learned drawing from a M. Rochard, who had seen both his own parents go to the guillotine. The young Mérimée growing up in post-revolution Paris with parents as intelligent as his, could scarcely be unaware of the grimness and brutality of life. It was the first century of European democracy, and Mérimée was a democrat, though not a simple or steadfast one, for he had Napoleonic sympathies and became the friend of the Comtesse de Montijo, the Empress Eugénie's mother; he was touched with the same pitch as that family of adventurers, the Bonapartes. Just as the ponderous oddities of the Hanoverian court had fascinated Walpole, so the adventitious volcanic splendours of the Second Empire suited Mérimée's tastes and abilities as a chronicler. Against the background of eighteenth-century England his volatility would have seemed lacking in integrity. But for all that, Mérimée was less of a dilettante than Walpole. Letter-writing excepted, everything that Walpole did, Mérimée could do better. The measure of their talents is *Colomba* and *The Castle of Otranto*, the measure of their knowledge, the building of Strawberry Hill on the one hand and the restoration of Laon cathedral on the other. For while Walpole played with a Gothicism half his own invention, Mérimée as Inspector-General of Monuments did an almost invaluable service to France in the preservation and restoration of her Roman remains and of some of her finest cathedrals and churches. The son of a drawing-master and the friend of artists and architects, he knew the difference between the true and the false, between style and no style. Walpole—alas!—the son of a Prime Minister, had no such friends and he could seldom distinguish between style and no style. But even so it is unnecessary to pay too great homage to Mérimée's taste as opposed to Walpole's; Mérimée found something so grand and so simple about the Crystal Palace that he declared it had to be seen to be understood. He jeered at it—"c'est un joujou qui coûte vingt-cinq millions, et une cage où plusieurs grandes églises pourraient valser"—but he was dazzled, as he was dazzled by the prospect of a chair in the French Academy and by the Second Empire.[1]

The formality and stability of the eighteenth century no longer existed. In 1810 Napoleon had married the Archduchess Marie Louise, and Queen Charlotte, until then unperturbed by all she had seen and heard, took a pound of snuff in an hour "exclaiming between each pinch 'My Got! my Got! what will this come to?—the oldest House in Europe married to an Emperor of yesterday. My Got! my Got! married to *nothing*, he has no blood in his veins.'"[2] Her intuitions were correct, it was the beginning of many things, of a century full of strange, melodramatic events, and unimagined changes in thought and ways of life. It was perfectly typical of the nineteenth century that Mérimée should meet in a coach a Spanish nobleman of old family who had made a love match

[1] Fitzgerald thought the Crystal Palace one of the best things the century had produced. It must have supplied a need to the nineteenth-century mind and eye of which the twentieth century is not conscious.

[2] Quoted by Lady Bessborough in a letter to Lord Granville, May 1810.

with a Miss Kirkpatrick, " riche à millions et belle comme le jour," who claimed descent from Finn MacCumhail, the father of Usheen, better known in literature as Ossian; that this Miss Kirkpatrick as the Comtesse de Montijo and mother of two charming children should become one of Mérimée's closest friends, and Mérimée her confidant even in the matter of the marriage of the spirited younger daughter Eugénie. It was rumoured and has never been authoritatively denied, that Mérimée wrote the letters which Eugénie sent to the unsavoury Louis Napoleon during her courtship. At least he was cognisant of all the stages that led up to the most spectacular marriage of the century—a marriage which filled the *señoritas* with such envy that they fell into hysterics and demanded to be taken to Paris, since there was clearly no future for a young person in Spain.

At least one can say that Mérimée would have been quite capable of writing Eugénie de Montijo's love-letters. There was a small thread of duplicity woven into his character; without it he could scarcely have piloted himself through the varying depths and shallows of his frequently contemporaneous intrigues. He said once that his only hypocrisy consisted in hiding from the people he loved all the ill they did him; nevertheless he spared Jenny Dacquin pangs of jealousy—and himself reproaches—by converting the *chapelière* who took pity on him in the floods at Perpignan into a *chapelier*. He economised his amiability, making the same compliment satisfy two friends, and he had recourse to the finesses without which few men have conducted successfully an elaborate public and private career. If the honesty of Walpole shines out by comparison with this, one must remember that Walpole lived a great part of his life in country retirement upon a very comfortable income from Government sinecures. And there are degrees and varieties of honesty. Walpole understood his own psychology too little to be deeply honest; he lived before the Deluge and Mérimée lived after it, and bore perpetual witness to it by his informed mind and his conscious and complicated personality.

Mérimée's best-known letters, those to Jenny Dacquin, his *Inconnue*, the young woman who threw herself at his head in so odd a manner, have not yet been published either completely or in their correct order, and until they are it is not possible to give a final judgment upon them. In their present truncated and disordered condition they are inferior in interest to the *Lettres à Mme de Montijo*, and it is very possible that these will always be the crown of Mérimée's correspondence. To be at his best a letter-writer must find in his correspondent a mind and personality able to rise or fall to whatever level he may seek, receptive to the same degree that he is expansive. With Jenny Dacquin, Mme de Rochejacquelein, and Panizzi, Mérimée adjusted himself and made selections from the contents of his mind. With Mme de Montijo one feels that he simply threw open the lock gates, knowing that all he had to tell of himself, Paris, politics, gossip, ideas, would flow smoothly into her mind and find a just welcome and appreciation.

Like everyone who feels intensely, he believed that there was value in feeling intensely. Nothing, he said to Jenny Dacquin, was worse than the life of an oyster, even of an oyster that is never eaten. Of his many affairs one at least meant so much to him that when his mistress Mme Delessert (having taken another lover) abandoned him without explanation at the end of a twenty years' liaison, the whole of the past was poisoned for him. He felt himself robbed, stripped, left for dead; even his memories were destroyed, and for years inspiration deserted him. He did not make a secret of this to Mme de Montijo or even to Mme de la Rochejacquelein. The life of the emotions was immensely important to him and he did not dream of anything so unnatural as denying his emotions expression among intimate and trustworthy friends. When his American friend Mr. Childe lost his wife, Mérimée found his self-restraint terrible to see. "Vous savez le défaut de la race saxonne," he said, " c'est de paraître *manly*." Nevertheless, to the world at large he chose to be inscrutable, with such success that even to-day, when thousands of his letters are before the public, the nature of the most essential relationships of his life is still in dispute. But about his feelings in general he leaves us in as little doubt as Mme du Deffand did, and his complaint is essentially hers.

" What is this world? What axen man to have?
Now with his love, now in his colde grave."

He detested old age. " Il me semble que je sens tout ce que je sentais à vingt-cinq ans. Quelle triste chose que l'âme ne vieillesse pas en même temps que le corps."[1] It might be Mme du Deffand speaking. Like her he found the widespread habit of going to bed at night insufferable; the night was made for talking—an opinion which was probably strengthened in him by the study of Russian novels, for Mérimée was one of the first European men of letters to learn and appreciate Russian. It would be easy to collect a score of passages that seem echoes of Mme du Deffand but are simply Mérimée revealing what he feels at the bottom of his heart. "Le monde est devenu plus bruyant et plus vide que jamais. Je ne m'y amuse plus du tout et il me semble que les autres ne s'y amusent guère." "Mais décidément je prends en horreur la vie de Paris et les Parisiens. Je songe très sérieusement à m'en aller quelque part bien loin, laisser mes os dans quelque pays favorisé du soleil, comme les vieux chats qui abandonnent la maison quand ils se sentent malades. J'ai perdu presque tous mes amis, je suis parfaitement inutile aux autres, et je m'ennuie."[2] And yet just as Mme du Deffand went on entertaining her friends in spite of her disillusionment and boredom, so Mérimée paid his visits and went to court long after he was tired. There was always for Mme du Deffand the chance that her guests might bring her a morsel of news worth passing on to Walpole, and Mérimée always hoped that he might pick up the story of some *bêtise* to amuse Mme de Montijo, exiled to Spain by her prudent son-in-law. For instance, there was the

[1] Mérimée to Mme de Montijo, July 15th, 1858.
[2] *Ditto*, May 7th, 1853.

story of Walewski (disconsolate because Rachel had shut her doors upon him) accepting the invitation of a lady at the Scala in Milan who had mistaken him for an old lover, he in his turn supposing the lady to be an old mistress forgotten. " Enfin," says Mérimée, " après que la dame lui eut pardonné tout ce qu'il était possible de pardonner, Walewski lui dit: '—Mais pourquoi donc m'appelez-vous toujours Alexandre? Je m'appelle Napoleon Walewski.' "[1] Certain of Mérimée's acquaintances endeared themselves greatly to him by their gift for *bêtises*; there was M. de Rambuteau, who had difficulty in spelling but always wrote messages upon his visiting cards, to the Princesse de Ligne: " Je suis Vénus en personne," and to Mrs. Graham, whose child George had entertained him in her absence: " Votre gorge est admirable." There was Mme de Péreuse, famous for her ingenuousness. " On se marie beaucoup," she had said, " surtout les femmes," and explaining the success of a friend in getting whatever she wanted from ministers: " Elle a tant d'entrejambe " (meaning *entregent*). But if M. de Rambuteau or Mme de Péreuse failed to provide Mérimée with sport, there was always the latest Parisian hypocrisy. In the Spring of 1843 he writes to the Comtesse de Montijo that all the women are converted and writing books of devotion instead of immoral novels. " Ce n'est guère plus amusant." Mme de Ludre had produced two volumes on dogma, in one of which she declared that it was wrong to damn oneself for the sake of a pleasure which lasted only

[1] Mérimée to Mme de Montijo, April 12th, 1846.

sixteen minutes. " On se perd en conjectures sur ce chiffre." Prudery he hated. In the *Lettres à une Inconnue* he describes his difficulties with the proofs of Prince Galitzin's translation of Tourgenieff's *Smoke*. Galitzin's neo-catholicism had flinched at the meeting of the two lovers. Instead of " Deux heures après, Litvinof était seul sur son divan," he had written " Une heure après, Litvinof était dans sa chambre." Mérimée was intensely amused. " Vous voyez bien que c'est beaucoup plus moral, et que supprimer une heure, c'est diminuer le péché de moitié. Ensuite, chambre, au lieu de divan, est bien plus vertueux . . . j'ai rétabli les deux heures et le divan. . . ."[1]

As M. Filon has pointed out, while he was timid in his published works, he was often bold and confident in his letters, and in them until the end of his life he gave constant evidence of his culture and perspicacity. He not only grasped facts but he co-ordinated them. His generalisations bear re-reading and considering. He preferred, he said, ancient history to modern, because it was so much less ambiguous—modern history had always the two aspects, official and real. " Alexandre allait en Asie pour conquérir. Aujourd'hui on n'annexe pas un village sans assurer ses contemporains de son désintéressement."[2] Among the ancients he discriminated, having a great aversion for the Egyptians and their art. " L'esprit de suite des ouvriers égyptiens avait quelque chose de tuant pour

[1] Mérimée, *Lettres à une Inconnue*, September 27th, 1867.

[2] Mérimée to Mme de la Rochejacquelein (*Une Correspondance inédite*), May 10th, 1860.

la pensée. On me dit qu'on ne connait pas de vers dans leur langue. Ils ont vécu des milliers d'années sans imagination."[1] His letters are full of such acuteness. He remarked to Mme de la Rochejacquelein that while he met at every step in the Transtevere heads of which one could see the copies in marble at the Vatican, yet there was a difference in character between the present-day Italian and the Italian of early times which was difficult to fathom. " Nous sommes, au contraire, les mêmes Gaulois qui prirent le Capitole et furent mis en déroute par des oies. . . ."[2] He took pains to discover the true characters of nations. His letters to Panizzi are full of penetrating comments upon England and the English. " John Bull, quand il a eu peur, est impitoyable." He observed that the Queen of the Netherlands had the German idea of vivacity, namely to throw oneself out of the window " pour avoir l'air dégagé." Lord Shaftesbury's speech in Parliament on the Druses amused him very much. Lord Shaftesbury made out the Druses to be charming creatures, merely goaded to massacre Christians because the Emperor had sent them Catholic instead of Protestant missionaries. Mérimée took the first opportunity that came of asking Lord Shaftesbury if he had read M. de Sacy on the Druses. He had never so much as heard of the book, and was " un peu époufflé " when Mérimée told

[1] Mérimée à Mme de la Rochejacquelein, December 27th, 1859.

[2] The Roman geese were favourites with Mérimée. In 1859 he wrote to Panizzi : " Ce qu'il y a de certain, c'est que les descendants de Brennus ne sont guère d'humeur à prendre le Capitole, n'y eût-il que leurs anciennes ennemies les oies pour le garder."

him that the Druses adored " le *grim gentleman below*."[1] He held that if Turks were prevented from violating Greek and Bulgarian Christians, Greek and Bulgarian Christians would violate Turks " car dans ce pays-là on viole toujours."

Mérimée's mind may seldom have fathomed any matter of great depth, but it never rested on the surface of anything. To ninety-nine persons in a hundred the name Sappho stands for a suitable subject for sculpture, or a symbol of the highest achievement, or the first woman pervert, or at the most for all three. Mérimée cannot refer to her without making a comment that strikes fire out of the stony problem of sexual inequality. " Voici une chose qui m'étonne: pourquoi les femmes, qui ont tant d'imagination ne sont-elles pas poètes ? Il y a bien Sappho, qui a fait la plus belle ode connue, quoique très immorale, mais ce n'était pas plus une femme que la vivandière des zouaves qui a tué tant d'Autrichiens."[2] His mind ranged; he weighed the massacre of St. Bartholomew and " les friponneries de maint actionnaire de chemin de fer en 1857 " and found little to choose between them. " L'idée que la vie d'un homme est *chose grave* est une idée toute moderne," he observed. But in spite of realising that it was a modern idea, and perhaps only an idea, Mérimée did himself feel that human life was *chose grave*. He was brought up in scepticism, by parents " chez qui la probité, le culte de l'honneur et la conscience remplacent aisément

[1] Mérimée to Mme de la Rochejacquelein, September 6th, 1860.
[2] *Ditto*, September 5th, 1859.

la foi,"[1] but in scepticism that gave far more consideration to the claims of Christian dogma than is customary among Christians themselves. It is curious to compare Walpole's " Dieu a fait tant de bon et de beau, qu'on devrait se fier à lui sur le reste " with Mérimée's reply to Mme de la Rochejacquelein when she tried to convert him:

" Je pense très souvent à Dieu et à l'autre monde, quelquefois avec espérance; d'autre fois avec beaucoup de doutes. Dieu me semble très probable, et le commencement de l'Evangile de saint Jean n'a rien qui me répugne. Quant à l'autre monde, j'ai bien plus de peine à y croire. Il m'est bien difficile de n'y pas voir une invention de la vanité humaine."[2]

Everything was more difficult for Mérimée than it was for Walpole. When his servant hanged himself after stealing from his master, Walpole showed himself a man of feeling and pity, but there is never any suggestion that the problem of human responsibility troubled him as it troubled Mérimée. As a juryman Mérimée knew that he would not hesitate to condemn any man that he believed guilty, but he said, setting it down once and for all in his quick, easy fashion, that he found human justice merely provisional, " si j'avais à donner ma voix au Jugement dernier, ce serait tout autre chose."

Dilettantism itself had grown a more serious affair since the eighteenth century passed out. The best minds of the nineteenth century may not compare very

[1] Trahard, *La Jeunesse de Mérimée.*

[2] Mérimée to Mme de la Rochejacquelein, November 7th, 1859.

favourably with the best minds of the eighteenth century, but undoubtedly the general level of intellectual life was higher. In England the graceful triflings of the *World* or the *Spectator* gave place to the weightier quarterly; criticism, the hybrid, gained a place for itself not very far below art on the one hand and philosophy on the other, while Germany and Russia began to contribute to European literature in general. Obviously one could not keep pace by mere placid absorption with the new literature and the growth in organised thought; the former entertainments of a gentleman of leisure had ceased to be suitable for a leisurely life. To make matters the more complicated, the age of invention had set in, and men were everywhere contriving to economise time, a policy which proved itself as fatal in a different field as hoarding gold, and brought on a universal time-famine. In Mérimée we see what a man of active and acute mind could do to make himself a master of the new situation. For Walpole the first question had never been more than this: What are the ten-score persons of distinction in England and France (no one else need concern us) thinking and saying and doing at the moment? Mérimée, without excluding that question, added a dozen more and was not content until he answered them. For part of his life he was extremely successful. In art, literature, history, politics and society he proved himself knowledgeable; he understood and perceived, he organised his information. He even wrote admirable books of his own. But in the latter part of his life the strain grew too great;

versatility became impossible. His hand grew heavy and he confined himself first to the production of careful unreadable historical works, and then abandoning that, devoted himself to philology. It was a comprehensible and logical end. He found intuitively the refuge of specialisation to which so many have fled since his day.

III

1. DOROTHY OSBORNE

2. MME DE SÉVIGNÉ

III

1. DOROTHY OSBORNE

CHRONOLOGICALLY Dorothy Osborne as a letter-writer must precede Mme de Sévigné. She was born, indeed, a year later than Mme de Sévigné and died a year earlier, but her correspondence with Sir William Temple took place before their marriage in 1654, while the greater part of the surviving letters of Mme de Sévigné were written after 1670. One always thinks of Mme de Sévigné as a widow—although neither the acquisition of the unsatisfactory Marquis de Sévigné at the age of eighteen, nor the loss of him at twenty-six, can have affected her very deeply—but Dorothy Osborne lives for posterity only as a girl. Of her forty-one years as Lady Temple we know only a few bare circumstances. We know that the Temples cultivated and valued family ties, and Dorothy's sister-in-law, Lady Giffard, declared that William's wife " fell into " the family " as naturally, as if she had been borne there." Of her nine children seven died in infancy, an adored daughter died of smallpox at fourteen and the remaining son drowned himself in 1689 at the age of twenty-five, a week after being made

Secretary at War.[1] One particular of her married life suggests that Lady Temple differed from the Dorothy Osborne who hated a crowd of company and said of London, " I . . . am soe litle taken with the place that I could sitt heer [in Bedfordshire] seven years without soe much as thinking once of goeing to it." Sir William Temple, so Lady Giffard says, had a house in Pall Mall " wholy for his Wife," and she was in the habit of going there while Sir William remained in the country. Altogether we know just enough about Lady Temple to suspect that Dorothy Osborne changed and developed along lines that brought her nearer to Mme de Sévigné, but their letters present to us an Englishwoman and a Frenchwoman almost wholly unlike.

Mme de Sévigné was a personage and a woman of the world. We compare her with Mme de Rambouillet, Mme de Maintenon, Mme du Deffand, with a tradition of women as remarkable socially as intellectually, who steered their lives through marital and extra-marital reefs, intrepid mistresses of every situation. Dorothy Osborne was far from being imprudent, but her prudence was a herb in the garden, the prudence of Mme de Sévigné, or Mme de Maintenon, the essence of that herb, distilled and preserved. In the life of Mme de Sévigné one can never go far without being reminded of some code—of manners,

[1] A note still exists written by him and endorsed by his mother : " Child's paper he writ before he killed himself." The reason of his suicide is supposed to have been anxiety over a private negotiation entered into on behalf of William of Orange, but in the note he said : " Having been long tired of the Burthen of this life, 'tis now become Insupportable," a curious echo of his mother's own melancholy, her wish for " an early, and a quiet grave, free from the trouble of this buissy world."

of morals, of ideas. Dorothy Osborne, without being in any way unconventional, gives an impression of freedom and individuality and isolation. Until she married, when we lose sight of her, she had experienced life in many of its separate constituents—danger, ambition, poverty, love, treachery—but she knew very little of life with those elements fused together, qualified and controlled by a dominating group of people. She was deep and sincere, and, to my knowing, the most charming person that has ever lived; yet limited, narrow, even uncivilised. In a sense there is very little in her letters, beyond her nonpareil self, while the whole world crowds into those of Mme de Sévigné.

But of all the differences between the two, the racial difference is the most striking and the most comprehensive. Their advantages of birth and education were similar, they were both more than usually intelligent and attractive, but Mme de Sévigné was a type of woman which no other country but France has bred; no English type compares with it or can compete with it. The names one might connect with Dorothy Osborne are Margaret Roper, Lady Jane Grey, Dorothy Wordsworth, none resembling her in the peculiar charm of her personality, but like her in simplicity and integrity and an unperishing freshness, in their loyalty and submission to all the ties of blood and marriage and their quiet independence of the world in general. When Dorothy Osborne found herself in a crowded house, where men and women of all ages discussed the relations of the sexes as perseveringly as in any other century, no one agreed with her ideas, but she was perfectly able to stand alone, only complaining to Temple that she could not " beat into theire head's a passion that must be subject to noe decay, an Even Perfect Kindnesse that must last perpetually." (Desdemona speaks, or Imogen.) She intimidated people—to her distress—by an appearance of stateliness and coldness; indeed, the eyes' sadness upon which her mother twitted her, give her face in the portrait at Broadlands a look of courteous disdain. It is hard to imagine her moving among people, mixing and dealing with them easily, compliantly, and accepting the social compromise as Mme de Sévigné did or any other woman of the world.

The " good motions " of her London relatives vexed Dorothy Osborne so much that she would live in a hollow tree, she said, to avoid them. But her dislike of people was not due to shyness, in so far as shyness means sensitiveness to the opinions and attitude of other people: she assured Temple that it concerned her no more whether she was thought handsome or ill-favoured, witty or stupid, than whether people thought her name was Elizabeth or Dorothy. Like Mme du Deffand she felt she did not belong to the world and had never been fashioned to suit it; in one of the most beautiful passages in her letters she wishes that she and Temple were out of it all.

" Doe you remember Arme[1] and the little house there ? shall wee goe thither ? that's next to being out of the worlde—there we might live like Baucis

[1] Herm, one of the Channel Islands.

and Philemon, grow old together in our litle Cottage and for our Charrity to some shipwrakt stranger obtaine the blessing of dyeing both at the same time. how idly I talk! tis because the Storry pleases mee, none in Ovide soe much. I remember I cryed when I read it, mee thought they were the perfectest Characters of a con[ten]ted marriage where Piety and Love were all theire wealth and theire poverty feasted the Gods where rich men shutt them out."[1]

To all her charm and humour she joined the singleness and steadfastness of mind and heart that mark the heroine of tragedy. She held a few things in life intensely important, worth staking all her happiness on. " Love," she said, speaking assuredly not from prudishness but from knowledge of passion, " Love is a Terrible word, and I should blush to death if any thing but a letter accused mee on't, pray bee merciful and lett it run friendship in my next Charge."[2]

We have considered the little that is known of Dorothy Osborne's married life, but not her history before the correspondence. It explains in part at least her character and her disposition, for uncertainty and hardship ruled all her early life. When she was born her ancestors had been men of culture holding government offices for nearly a hundred years. Her great-grandfather had married the niece of Sir John Cheke, had begotten twenty-two children and given his advice on matters of trade and finance to Queen Elizabeth. Sir Peter Osborne, her father, was a Royalist and

[1] Dorothy Osborne to William Temple, January 13th-15th, 1653/4.
[2] *Ditto*, September 3rd, 1653.

Lieutenant-Governor of Guernsey, and held Castle Cornet for the King when the Civil War broke out, suffering great privations through the treachery of Colonel Carteret in Jersey. For two years Dorothy and her mother lived at St. Malo, endeavouring with their vanishing resources to send supplies to the besieged Sir Peter, and after he had retired to St. Malo Dorothy and one of her brothers visited him there. On their way they met another young royalist, William Temple, who was starting on his travels, glad to see the last of his tutor at Emmanuel (for he always preferred tennis to logic). The well-known escapade in the Isle of Wight must have helped to bring their chance friendship to its quick maturity. This was in 1648, the marriage not until the end of 1654, and in between came privation, separation, and frequent despair. Dorothy returned from France with her ruined father, herself " growne heavy," so she said, " and sullen, froward and discomposed." In England they lived at Chicksands, a Gilbertine monastery in Bedfordshire, and it was from Chicksands, founded in Henry I's reign, five centuries old and probably half ruined by the middle of the seventeenth century, that Dorothy wrote almost all her letters to Temple. She had seen enough of poverty at St. Malo and refused to consider a marriage that could not be placed on a sound financial basis and countenanced by both families. In all the discussion of her marriage and the long disputed marriage settlement she showed considerable worldly wisdom and what she would have called " sober councell." The chief enemy of the lovers was

Dorothy's brother Henry, whose mind was set upon his sister's making a wealthy match, who when roused would bring up again "upon the Stage" all the suitors she had refused—"like Richard the 3ds Ghosts to reproach mee withall." Henry was not so dull as the diary which he left behind might suggest. From Dorothy's letters we discover that he had a habit of coming out of his surly shell at night over the fire and discussing such topics as the future of flying with Mr. Gibson, a neighbouring clergyman and a friend of his, and Dorothy, who had been dreaming and not listening, pricked up her ears at this and asked them to tell her more as she had missed the beginning of their discussion. But as they only laughed at her we do not know why a couple of country gentlemen decided over a fire in the autumn of 1653 "that people might fly like Birds and dispatch theire Journey's soe." It was in the following February that Dorothy quarrelled with Henry for saying that Temple considered neither religion nor honour, only his own advancement, and they "parted in great Anger with the Usuall Ceremony of a Leg and a Courtesy." On these terms they continued until the next evening, and then after everyone else had gone to bed they sat in silence for half an hour.

"At Last in a pittifull Tone, Sister say's hee, I have heard you say that when any thing troubles you, of all things you aprehend goeing to bed, because there it increases upon you and you lye at the mercy of all your sad thoughts which ye silence and darknesse of ye night adds a horror to; I am at that passe now, I vow to God I would not indure another night like the last to gaine a Crowne."[1]

Dorothy turned this appeal aside with a casual reference to the Spleen, but from that she started "a discourse of Melancholy and ye Causes" and presently they were discussing religion as peaceably and charitably as "two hermitts . . . in a Cell they Equaly inhabitt," begging one another's pardon, promising abstinence from carping and criticising in the future.

When the correspondence with Temple began, in 1652, Sir Peter Osborne was almost wholly an invalid, tended by Dorothy, who wrote more than once from his sick-room, where she sat all night with "a poore moaped fellow" who waited on her father. He died in the Spring of 1654, Lady Osborne having died three or four years earlier. The guests of the Osbornes at Chicksands were mainly such as one would expect in a house of bereavement, sickness, and broken fortunes. "Two dumbe Gentlemen" arrive and interrupt Dorothy's letter to Temple. "I am soe tyred with makeing of sign's and tokens for everything I had to say, good god, how doe those that live always with them?"[2] Or a widowed cousin came for a couple of days and Dorothy for lack of conversation "gott her to Card's, and then with a great deal of patience lost my money to her." In the middle of the play the carrier came with one of Temple's letters, but courtesy and the presence of Henry made it necessary to sit

[1] Dorothy Osborne to William Temple, February 4th, 1653/4.
[2] *Ditto*, October 23rd, 1653.

until she could make the excuse of going to fetch more money. " I did not make such hast back againe I can assure you, I took time enough to have Coyned my self some money if I had had the Art on't, and left my Brother enough to make all his addresses to her, if hee were soe disposed."[1]

In the circumstances it is not surprising that Dorothy frequently suffered from a " Scurvy Spleen." She went to Epsom to drink the waters in the hope of alleviating her sufferings, and even drank an infusion of steel in white wine every morning, playing " Shutle cock " for an hour or two afterwards. Constitutionally she was not gay, she speaks of her " owne naturall dull humour " as unalterable, but not signifying sadness. The Osborne blood may have had something to do with it. Dorothy describes her eldest sister, Elizabeth, as " a melancholy retir'd woman " who never sought any other company but that of her husband and her books. Almost all the reflections upon life in Dorothy's letters take their tone from the settled and calm melancholy of a person of heroic cast whose early years have been full of " contrariety's." Occasionally from melancholy she passes to bitterness almost as strong as any Mme du Deffand expressed in her old age. Of her cousin Mrs. Franklin, who had married for money, she wrote in December 1653, at a moment when matters were very difficult between her and Temple:

" Shee's happyer by much than I shall ever bee, but I doe not envy her, may she long injoy it, and I, an

[1] Dorothy Osborne to William Temple, March 5th, 1652/3.

H

early, and a quiet grave, free from the trouble of this buissy world, where all with passion persue theire owne interests at theire Neighbours Charges, where nobody is pleased but somebody complain's ont, and where tis impossible to bee without giveing and receiving injury's."

This again, barring the confidence in future glory, is the corollary of Mme du Deffand's " Dites-moi, pourquoi, détestant la vie, je redoute la mort ? "

" Wee complaine of this world and the Variety of Crosses and afflictions it abound's in, and yet for all this whoe is weary on't (more then in discourse) ? whoe thinks with pleasure of leaveing it, or preparing for the next ? Wee see olde folkes that have outlived all ye comforts of life, desyre to continue it, and nothing can wean us from the ffolly of preffering a mortall beeing subject to great infirmity's and unavoydable decays, before an immortall one and all ye Glorry's that are promised with it."[1]

But unlike Mme du Deffand, unlike anyone but Dorothy Osborne, she follows all this great seriousness with a threat that Temple shall have no more preaching from her because it is too good for him—he is not " mortified Enough " to benefit by it. The not infrequent moralising in her letters is always saved either by such humour, turning upon herself, or by the sincerity of her feelings and the absence of anything second hand or commonplace. If inconstancy is the subject she does not turn up the hem of her argument with any quotation or claptrap, but with a story about

[1] Dorothy Osborne to William Temple, February 4th, 1653/4.

" a Gentlewoman in this Country " who had suffered so upon the death of her husband no one thought she would live and now was " passionatly taken again wth another."[1] If happiness is the subject, and Temple has said that she might have been happy without him if she had resolved to be so, she questions it with gentle shrewdness; if one might be happy by resolving to be so " twere not soe hard a thing to get as tis believ'd."[2]

Her humour was the dry and seasoned sort much less rare in melancholy than in cheerful people, a drollness in her ideas, a quick observing eye, a subtle, witty tongue and—with those she loved—something of the impudence of Beatrix. " What think you ? " she writes at the end of a long letter in January 1653/4 when Temple is on the point of leaving for Ireland, " have I not don faire for once ? would you wish a longer letter ? see how kinde I grow at parting, whoe would not goe into Ireland to have such another ? " Her belief in " an Even Perfect Kindnesse that must last perpetually " did not prevent her complaining of Lord Broghill's[3] romance *Parthenissa*, that the ladies in it were " all soe kinde they make noe sport." And kind as she was herself, she was never too much so to make a little sport of human absurdities. The wife of her brother " Pe " was, she explained to Temple, " though a very good woman, the most troublesome one in a Coach that ever was, wee dare not let our tongues lye more on one side of our mouths

[1] Dorothy Osborne to William Temple, December 16th, 1653.
[2] *Ditto*, October 1653.
[3] Better known as the Earl of Orrery, his title after the Restoration.

than tother for fear of overturning it."[1] The carrier had brought her one of Temple's letters with a broken seal and was so grieved at her suspicion " that hee has neither eate nor slept (to do him any good) since he came home." Walker the goldsmith, who was setting a seal for her, annoyed her by his lack of invention. " It makes mee think of the fellow that could paint nothing but a flower de luce, whoe when he mett with one that was so firmly resolved to have a Lyon for his signe that there was noe perswading him out ont, Well say's the painter, let it bee a Lyon then but it shall bee as like a flower de Luce as ere you saw, soe because you would have it a dolphin he consented to it but it is liker an ilfavoured knot of riban."[2]

The letters, moreover, are full of little real things such as escape all but the most delicate and natural minds, those fragments which recreate something so much larger than themselves, tiny mirrors that reflect great rooms, four-inch windows that look out on half a county. She caught and preserved as only rare and original writers can the interstitial acts and emotions of life. So she describes how she chid her maid for waking her in the morning but was silenced by hearing there were letters, and in her impatience could not get out of bed but told the girl to tie up the curtains to let in the light; and with that little detail about the curtains the scene, slight and unimportant as it is, becomes unforgettable.

Enough has been quoted to make even the reader

[1] Dorothy Osborne to William Temple, July 15th, 1654.
[2] *Ditto*, October 1653.

who does not know her letters at first hand perceive that Dorothy Osborne had singular gifts of expression. Her style, like herself, is simple and yet not so simple. She sometimes ends a letter as the Elizabethans ended their sonnets with a conceit gracefully linked.

"I believe I shall live heer till there is quite a new Language spoke where you are, and shall come out like one of the Seven Sleepers, a Creature of another Age—but tis noe matter, soe you understande mee, though nobody else doe, when I say how much I am

Your faithfull "[1]

But the more familiar her letters become to the reader the more the words seem to fall not in any considered design but in the folds that her thoughts gave them, and warm from her mind. Nothing could be more dateless in manner than this: "I think I need not tell you how dear you have been to me nor that in your kindness I placed all the satisfaction of my life."[2] Indeed on simplicity and clearness of style she had strong and definite views, sympathising with an old uncle of hers who threw the standish at the head of a manservant to whom he was dictating a letter, for presuming to replace his plain words with an elegant periphrasis. For real trenchancy of expression Dorothy, when roused, has no equal in her own sex; she is better than even Mme du Deffand, less abstract and more picturesque. "I wonder," she wrote to Temple from Knowlton in Kent, "with what confidence you can complaine of my short Letters that are soe

[1] Dorothy Osborne to William Temple, August 5th, 1653.
[2] *Ditto*, December 8th, 1653.

guilty your self in the same kinde. I have not seen a Letter this month, y^{t} has been above half a sheet; never trust me if I write more than you, that live in a desolated Country[1] where you might ffinish a Romance of ten Tomes before any body interrupted you; I that live in a house the most filled of any since ye Arke, and where I can assure [you ?] one has hardly time for the most necessary occasion's."[2] Here, as in everything she wrote, we find her own sureness of manner and poise, derived not from sophistication but from her inward clearness and sanity. The quality of her mind and character penetrated all her actions and words, relating them to herself and to one another, so that one cannot take an episode from her life or a sentence from her letters without finding in it the meaning and grace peculiar to herself. This is the ultimate beauty of human personality, not built from any known virtues, a secret like the secret of poetry.

[1] Ireland.

[2] Dorothy Osborne to William Temple. July 10th, 1654.

2. MME DE SÉVIGNÉ

Dorothy Osborne describing her life to William Temple selected only a detail here and another there, the tying up of the curtains round her bed, the smell of the jasmine in the garden at night; but she wrote in a manner so finely expressive that, while we must always remain conscious of her natural reticence, we feel that we have been received into her confidence. In Mme de Sévigné's style on the other hand there is nothing that suggests reticence. Whatever she knows she tells with an explicitness, an assurance and a fullness that reflects her own bountiful personality. Spontaneous, prodigal, she treated the business of writing with the light-heartedness of the amateur—"C'est une si jolie chose que de savoir écrire ce que l'on pense." Not for her a long, sweating apprenticeship hardly forgotten even when mastery came. Edward Fitzgerald did not exaggerate when he said of her letters—quoting Kitty Clive on Mrs. Siddons—"It's all Truth and Daylight."

Her style is one of the mysteries of literature, for while it possesses the greatest refinement and sophistication, polish and wit, its basis is simply that of a nursery rhyme, the adding of statement to statement, the stringing together of large bright beads of facts.

"Le comte d'Estrées . . . a conté qu'en son voyage de Guinée il se trouva parmi des chrêtiens. Il y trouva une église, il y trouva vingt chanoines nègres tout nus avec des bonnets carrés et une aumusse au bras gauche, qui chantoient les louanges de Dieu."[1]

This is complete, and in its small way perfect. To add anything to it, one might suppose, would ruin it, to emphasise a single point would be fatal. But Mme de Sévigné cannot leave it alone; she must repeat, must emphasise, must amplify, and she does it with such skill that nothing is ruined; all the beads stand out larger and brighter than before.

"Il vous prie de réfléchir," she continues, "sur cette rencontre, et de ne pas croire qu'ils eussent le moindre surplis, car ils étoient comme quand on sort du ventre de sa mère, et noirs comme des diables. Voilà ma commission."

Nursery literature—like the literature of the half-civilised communities with which it is so closely connected—very easily conduces to gruesomeness, and at times the letters of Mme de Sévigné tend the same way. She wrote to her daughter in 1672 describing her dying aunt in a way so mercilessly clear and complete that the letter is almost too horrible to read.[2]

[1] Mme de Sévigné to Mme de Grignan, March 20th, 1671.

[2] "Elle est debout, c'est à dire dans sa chaise, avec sa robe de chambre, sa cornette, une coiffe noire par-dessus, et ses gants. Nulle senteur, nulle malpropreté dans sa chambre ; mais son visage est plus changé que si elle étoit morte depuis huit jours. Les os lui percent la peau ; elle est entièrement étique et desséchée ; elle n'avale qu'avec des difficultés extrêmes ; elle a perdu la parole. . . ." Mme de Sévigné to Mme de Grignan, June 24th, 1672.

Tender and affectionate as Mme de Sévigné was, nothing that could overtake humanity really appalled her. She had the hardy, unemotional sympathy of the professional nurse for the sick and the dying, and she described the bones piercing the skin in a dying woman with the same sort of tranquil satisfaction in doing her duty by the scene as she might have shown in describing the complexion of the bride at a marriage feast. In one sense there is no lack of imagination—in her aunt's death she foresaw her own:

". . . Cela nous creva le cœur, et nous fit voir qu'on joue longtemps la comédie, et qu'à la mort on dit la vérité. Je ne vous dis plus, ma fille, le jour de mon départ. . . ."

Her emotional reactions were far blunter and far narrower in scope than her perceptions, and her interests were almost too many for her to make profound distinctions between them. Youth interested her, death interested her, the way a human being passed from youth to age without really observing it, that fascinated her; it was one of the miracles of Providence that excited her special admiration. But she never saw youth as Shakespeare saw it, or death with Donne's eyes, or growing old with Tolstoy's.

But whatever her limitations, Mme de Sévigné seems the most competent woman writer that has ever lived. Her relationship to language was one of complete ascendancy; she understood it (bewildering, tormenting, Protean) as a fashionable woman understands dress. She made phrases with the swiftness and dexterity and coolness of an accomplished modiste twisting a bow of ribbon or placing a flower; she borrowed and adopted expressions that pleased her with bold, unfailing taste and precision. " Il y a de certaines douleurs dont on ne doit point se consoler, ni revoir le monde: il faut tirer les verrous sur soi, comme disoit notre bon cardinal." One feels the self-assurance, the easy expansiveness, the sense of *chic*, not only in masterpieces of writing and wit such as the famous *Lettre des foins*[1] but almost anywhere that one cares to open her correspondence.

" Je veux, ma bonne, vous faire un petit dessous de cartes qui vous surprendra: c'est que cette belle amitié de Mme de Montespan et de son amie[2] qui voyage est une véritable aversion depuis près de deux ans: c'est une aigreur, c'est une antipathie, c'est du blanc, c'est du noir. . . ."[3]

See how she settles herself to unfold her tale, how she takes her time, how deliberately she delivers the matter piece by piece, how firmly she underlines the central point—" c'est une aigreur, c'est une antipathie, c'est du blanc, c'est du noir."

Her emotional reactions were blunter than her perceptions, but does that tally with her love for her daughter, Mme de Grignan ? Not altogether. One cannot doubt the depth of emotion in some of the countless protestations. " Je vous aime avec une tendresse si sensible que je n'ose y penser ; c'est un endroit si vif et si délicat dans mon cœur que tout est

[1] Mme de Sévigné to M. de Coulanges, July 22nd, 1671.
[2] Mme de Maintenon.
[3] Mme de Sévigné to Mme de Grignan, August 7th, 1675.

loin en comparaison." But the irritation " that eternal daughter of hers " has caused among her readers (let us remember, however, that exception of Mme du Deffand) would scarcely be so widespread if her offence were merely the common one of excessive motherly love. On Mme de Sévigné's own showing maternal love had less to do with her feeling for Mme de Grignan than inclination; she never voluntarily forewent her company without regret and out of consideration not for herself but for Mme de Grignan, but with everyone else " c'est par considération pour moi." On each separation Mme de Sévigné passed through and described an anguish so elaborate that one marvels at the physical strength that could survive it. She could not think (on such occasions) of Mme de Grignan without weeping, and she thought of her incessantly. This was gross infatuation; it repels us as no amount of ordinary maternal affection could. Her unctuous comments upon Mme de Grignan's letters, by their lack of humour and insight, in one of the most humorous and acute of women, confirm every suspicion of the sort. She was positively unbalanced about this dry stick of a girl. The triumph (she says) of Mme de Grignan's letter is her remarks upon the Jews, but since the Queen of France and Mme de Béthune failed to convert them, Mme de Grignan could not be expected to. La Brinvilliers has gone to the stake and " rien n'est si plaisant " as Mme de Grignan's remarks upon her, but really she need not be afraid of meeting her in Paradise. And so on. It is amusing to observe that one of the few occasions on which Mme de Sévigné cried out " O vanité des vanités! " occurred in describing a crowded wedding party where all the guests were too occupied in other matters to wait for the answers to their enquiries after Mme de Grignan's health. Normally her friends encouraged her to believe her daughter the most beloved and admired woman in France; to find that a few torches and gold suits, some jewels and a crush of carriages could impart indifference about Mme de Grignan's health, shocked the mother into one of her rare moments of bitterness and doubt.

In considering Mme de Sévigné's protestations of affection for her daughter—and also in considering her style—one must remember that a masque-like exaggeration of moods and experiences was a persistent fashion in the seventeenth century. This exaggeration, however, is no more to be confused with lack of control than are the gestures and expressions of a ballet dancer; nor does it necessarily signify insincerity, although it is difficult for us in the present generation, reading such a passage as the following, to credit either Mme de Longueville or Mme de Sévigné with deep feeling. Mme de Longueville has just heard of her son's death in the campaign of 1672.[1]

" Et là-dessus elle tombe sur son lit, et tout ce que la plus vive douleur put faire, et par des convulsions, et par des évanouissements, et par un silence mortel, et

[1] Her first question has been of a kind that makes at least one of the differences between that century and ours very clear. "Ah ! mon cher fils ! est-il mort sur-le-champ ? N'a-t-il pas eu un seul moment ? Ah mon Dieu ! quel sacrifice ! "

par des cris étouffés, et par des larmes amères, et par des élans vers le ciel, et par des plaintes tendres et pitoyables, elle a tout éprouvé."[1]

One is tempted, but without real grounds, to suspect Mme de Sévigné of slight cynicism. Possibly Mme de Longueville went through the paces of her mourning rather less in the grand manner than Mme de Sévigné's style of reporting suggests. For she was incapable of leaving anything to the imagination, incapable of touching the heart by an indirect revelation such as Dorothy Osborne's "T'is a sad thing when all on's happinesse is only that ye world dos not know you are miserable." Consequently we understand and enjoy her better when she leaves the real and the tragic alone and employs her art to describe pure comedy such as Mme de Brissac and her colic.

"Madame de Brissac avoit aujourd'hui la colique; elle etoit au lit, belle et coiffée à coiffer tout le monde. Je voudrois que vous eussiez vu l'usage qu'elle faisoit de ses douleurs, et de ses yeux, et des cris, et des bras, et des mains qui traînoiant sur la couverture, et les situations, et la compassion qu'elle vouloit qu'on eût: chamarrée de tendresse et d'admiration, je regardois cette pièce. . . ."[2]

Mme de Sévigné was acute to observe dramatic detail, slow to understand the quality of the emotional experience at the centre of the drama, if it were more than a piece of vanity or ambition or social intrigue. In the well-known letter[3] describing the suicide of

[1] Mme de Sévigné to Mme de Grignan, June 20th, 1672.
[2] *Ditto*, May 21st, 1676. [3] *Ditto*, April 26th, 1671.

Vatel during Louis XIV's visit to Chantilly in 1671, there is a remarkable example of her extreme sensibility to the circumstances and details of the event and her insensibility to the tragedy of the piece as a whole. She seizes all the minor points, first the insufficiency of the roast meat, then the failure of the fireworks, then the misunderstanding about the fish, and finally Gourville's lack of sympathy—we feel, and she admits, how all this fascinated her. Vatel's state of mind and the appalling violence he did himself receive almost perfunctory attention in comparison with the shortage of the roast—a shortage which did not prevent there being sufficient for the king's table and for twenty-three more tables—and the business of the fish, which began to arrive from all sides after poor Vatel had given himself the final stab.

But it is important to realise that Mme de Sévigné was not cold or incapable of imaginative sympathy; on the contrary the scope of her affections and interests was abnormal; so much so that it deceives, as a tumbler filled with water to the very brim will appear empty. She considered humanity as a whole with a generosity so ample that one seldom thinks of it except as an attribute of God. "He maketh his sun to rise on the evil and on the good and sendeth rain on the just and on the unjust." Mme de Sévigné had her prejudices, certainly, and she made her judgments—she was quite sure La Brinvilliers would not afflict Mme de Grignan by appearing in heaven—but she satisfied M. de la Rochefoucauld's idea of friendship "avec toutes ses circonstances et dépendances"; the countenance she turned upon human nature was habitually open, confident, benign. Everything that made for suspicion or even for diffidence between friends, she disliked, and jealousy she loathed. " Ne parlons point de cette passion; je la déteste: quoiqu'elle vienne d'un fonds adorable, les effets en sont trop cruels et trop haïssables." Many people loathe jealousy, envy, slander and suspicion, and loathing, yet discover them the more readily on every side. Mme de Sévigné loathed them with a regal contempt; she expunged them by her disapproval. She said: Never talk to me of jealousy, and no one dared to do so. Having once seen and known what she disliked, she cut it for ever afterwards. For her courage was of the kind that would plunge into activity, she said, but not endure danger passively; she could meet death if it came with the noise of trumpets, in excitement, in companionship. To watch big waves haggling for her body and come in a leisurely fashion within an inch of death—" je ne comprends pas comment on s'y peut exposer."

Dorothy Osborne, with all her strength and sweetness, was more troubled by the unpleasantness of humanity than Mme de Sévigné. She could not easily affront what she disliked and deny its existence and so she longed to hide from the world upon a little island in the Channel. As for Lady Bessborough, her life was made a nightmare by the persecution of the Prince of Wales and Sheridan, by her enemies and her slanderers; in her letters one seldom escapes from the atmosphere of dread—of skeletons in cupboards, the keys of which are stolen. All the sordid appointments of blackmail gather there, fear, guilt, cupidity and confidential friends turned enemies. Lady Bessborough was a charming, generous, open-hearted woman. What she lacked was Mme de Sévigné's talent or genius for destroying the unpleasant. The wholesomeness of Mme de Sévigné's life was more than a personal attribute, it extended to everything she saw with her eyes or considered with her mind. Her nature was an ocean so large and so rich in purifying salts that all the sewage of the world could not pollute it.

Some people thrive on comfort and some on discomfort, and seem to attract either comfort or discomfort by an inner magnetism or their psychical economy. How seldom Mrs. Carlyle went upon a journey and found anything but terrors by the way—noise, dirt, hard beds, bugs. Mme de Sévigné on her way to Les Rochers is housed "comme une vraie princesse de Tarante, dans une belle chambre meublée d'un beau velours rouge cramoisi, ornée comme à Paris," where she finds "un bon lit où j'ai dormi admirablement, une bonne femme qui est ravie de m'avoir, une bonne amie qui a des sentiments dont vous seriez contente."[1] But one can grow almost as weary of Mme de Sévigné's satisfaction as of Mrs. Carlyle's dissatisfaction. And to attain her enviable condition, undoubtedly Mme de Sévigné juggled with some facts and did not discriminate too finely between others. With her appetite for all types of people, her enormous interest in life—as Mme du Deffand unkindly but truly said, her enormous interest in everything which had nothing

[1] Mme de Sévigné to Mme de Grignan, May 11th, 1689.

at all to do with her—her willingness to take things as they came, not anxious to examine too closely, her lack of fastidiousness and depth, combined moreover with a certain docility and resignation due to her sex and the age as well as to her disposition, Mme de Sévigné would have been satisfied with almost any sort of world, and was blissfully content with a very indifferent one.

" Mlle du Plessis est à son couvent; vous ai-je dit comme elle a joué l'affligée, et comme elle voloit la cassette, pendant que sa mère expiroit ? Vous ririez de voir comme tous les vices et toutes les vertus sont jetés pêle-mêle dans le fond de ces provinces; car je trouve des âmes de paysans plus droites que des lignes, aimant la vertu, comme naturellement les chevaux trottent. La main qui jette tout cela dans son univers, sait fort bien ce qu'elle fait, et tire sa gloire de tout, et tout est bien."[1]

" Cela est dans l'ordre, et dans l'ordre de Dieu," runs the refrain to everything. If things go badly, so one learns to suffer, and can admire the docility of one's spirit; if they go well, so much the better, but one knows of course it cannot be for long. " Il faut s'attendre aux incommodités ordinaires de l'humanité; Dieu est le maître, je suis soumise à ses volontés." For Mme de Sévigné Providence filled the place that Mme du Deffand hoped Walpole might fill for her. " Pour ma Providence je ne pourrois pas vivre au paix, si je ne la regardois souvent; elle est la consolation des tristes états de la vie, elle abrège toutes les

[1] Mme de Sévigné to Mme de Grignan, June 21st, 1680.

plaintes, elle calme toutes les douleurs, elle fixe toutes les pensées. . . ."[1]

When her aunt grew critically ill just as Mme de Sévigné was about to leave Paris to visit her daughter, she could not help admiring the "contre-poids" which God placed against her pleasure. "Ah! que voilà bien le monde!" she exclaimed, sadly, but also complacently, and even with a tinge of waggishness such as old ladies have in discussing together human frailties. Mme de Sévigné knew the ways of Providence inside out.

She saw the universe not as the Stoics or the Epicureans had seen it and not in any sense as Christ saw it, but as a sublime compromise, and being a woman of the world, sane to the tips of her fingers, she understood, accepted and appreciated a compromise whenever she met it. Life inspired her with no fear and with little reverence; it was something to use, to manipulate and to enjoy. She watched the Spring come at Les Rochers and remarked that if need be she could quite well make a Spring. God indeed was master of *la haute couture* in such matters as a Spring, but he could not hide his secrets from an eye like hers, and her fingers itched to copy his work—to do more, to improve upon it. She considered the delightfulness of having singing leaves upon her trees; it seemed a curious error of taste that owls should be given voices when leaves were not. When the young Bishop of Léon died she perceived his removal to another world in intellectual terms so simple, that she seems to pluck

[1] Mme de Sévigné to Mme de Grignan, July 13th, 1689.

the whole purport of intellect, like a flower on a branch, to put it in the bosom of her dress and pass on.

"Je crois présentement que l'opinion *léonique* est la plus assurée: il voit de quoi il est question, ma bonne, et si la matière raisonne ou ne raisonne pas, et quelle sorte de petite intelligence Dieu a donnée aux bêtes, et tout le reste. Vous voyez bien que je le crois dans le ciel. . . ."[1]

"Et tout le reste," she says, half conscious—having read Pascal—that this is childishness, half in impatience, for these problems really mattered so little. They never weighed upon her nor intimidated her. Hence the lightness of touch which is one of her greatest charms. "La petite Mousse a une dent de moins, et ma petite-fille une dent de plus: ainsi va le monde." As if a Beethoven Sonata were adapted for harpsichord performance. This is a habit of mind not uncommon amongst women, this making sport of the immense affair, Life, by showing the march of time comprehended in the loss of a tooth in one mouth and the growth of a tooth in another. So Mrs. Carlyle two centuries later, ending a letter to her husband, wrote: "The canary continues to tumble off its perch, and I to lift it up! What a blessing to have somebody to always lift one up when one falls off the perch!"[2] Mme de Sévigné would have added a word of admiration for Providence whose whole functioning was mirrored in this continuing to lift up the canary, which continued to fall off its perch.

[1] Mme de Sévigné to Mme de Grignan, September 30th, 1671.
[2] Mrs. Carlyle to Thomas Carlyle, July 9th, 1858.

Her boast that she could make a Spring at any time if the need arose was of course only her way of making quite clear with what fascinated attention she had watched the Spring come at Les Rochers. So precise, curious and loving an observer of the details of life was inevitably more often analytic than synthetic, but many times she related the detail to the whole with such understanding of the processes of nature that the effect is synthetic—close indeed to creative. Take for example the letter upon growing old, written to the Président de Moulceau upon his becoming a grandfather, she herself being then over sixty.

" Je pourrois finir ici ma lettre, n'étant à autre fin; mais je veux vous demander par occasion comme vous vous portez d'être grand-père. Je crois que vous avez reçu une gronderie que je vous fais sur l'horreur que vous me témoigniez de cette dignité: je vous donnois mon exemple et vous disois: ' Pétus, non dolet.'[1] En effet, ce n'est point ce que l'on pense: la Providence nous conduit avec tant de bonté dans tous ces temps différents de notre vie, que nous ne les sentons quasi pas; cette pente va doucement, elle est imperceptible: c'est l'aiguille du cadran que nous ne voyons pas aller. Si à vingt ans on nous donnoit le degré de supériorité dans notre famille, et qu'on nous fît voir dans un miroir le visage que nous avons ou que nous aurons à soixante ans, en le comparant à celui de vingt, nous tomberions à la renverse, et nous aurions peur de cette figure; mais c'est jour à jour que nous avançons; nous sommes aujourd'hui comme hier, et demain

[1] *Sic*.

comme aujourd'hui; ainsi nous avançons sans le sentir, et c'est un des miracles de cette Providence que j'adore."[1]

This tranquil comprehension of one's own life in the span is one of the rarest of human faculties. Compared with this passage any remark of Mme du Deffand or of Mérimée upon the horror of the living mind within the decaying body seems tenuous and insufficient. And yet on many occasions Mme de Sévigné's homœopathy sounds like the fondest superstitions of old women in comparison with the clean, ruthless surgery of Mme du Deffand. For Mme de Sévigné had a gusto for living, and in that gusto is comprehended the best and the worst of her. To the cynic, she appears foolish and to the unhappy, superficial, and it is significant that the two English letter-writers whose admiration for her did not rest on this side of idolatry were men who (in very different ways) had ordered their lives to their own satisfaction—Horace Walpole and Edward Fitzgerald. The little inner circle of those who have manipulated fate sit admiring and understanding.

[1] Mme de Sévigné to the Président de Moulceau, January 27th, 1687.

IV

1. COWPER
2. LADY BESSBOROUGH
3. MRS. CARLYLE

IV

1. COWPER

DOROTHY OSBORNE at Chicksands led a quiet life, but Cowper at Olney, provided that we do not follow his mind into the places where it contemplated "the most tremendous subjects,"[1] led an even quieter one. His normal existence was absorbed in feminine and domestic trivialities, the arrival of a basket of fish and its acknowledgment, a visitor, a picnic, the care of his tame hares, sending instructions for a new hat to be made, not a "round slouch" but "a smart well-cocked fashionable affair," or requesting that "a genteelish tooth-pick case" might be found. To us to-day his interests seem few and pale. He read comparatively little, and current events seldom occupied his attention, unless a Bill came before Parliament which threatened to throw the lacemakers of Olney out of work. The circle of his friends and acquaintances was exceedingly small and select. His letters are almost the best example in English literature of how bricks may be made without straw. The supreme example is Jane Austen, and it cannot be a coincidence that her life overlapped Cowper's, and her experience

[1] See p. 139.

of genteel society in rural England was much the same as his.

Jane Austen's novels describe an existence in which ambition, passion, the arts, science, philosophy and politics are scarcely mentioned even in conversation, and in which literature and nature appear with all their pinion feathers plucked. Such a society as this did exist for a time in England in the late eighteenth and early nineteenth century, and in Cowper—in his sanity—we see a poet who was content to live inside such a nutshell and count himself a king of infinite space, but for his bad dreams. Just as the women in Jane Austen filled in their time with needlework and piano-playing and sketching, so Cowper to amuse himself became a carpenter, a gardener, and a bird-cage maker. Yet in the very midst of such playthings he would bring out a phrase which reminds us that he was a poet and his life a tragedy. "My days steal silently away, and march on (as poor mad King Lear would have made his soldiers march) as if they were shod with felt."

But let us set both the poet and the tragedy on one side, and consider in the meantime the little world that figures so largely in Cowper's letters.[1] Like Jane Austen's world it lies wedged between the struggle of the body for life and the struggle of the mind for truth. The first struggle has ended and the second not

[1] His letter to William Unwin (May 1784), describing the development of the friendship between Cowper and Mrs. Unwin and the Throckmortons, gives a perfect idea of this little world, and is well worth comparison with Jane Austen's work. As it is too long for the text or a footnote, I have given it in the appendix.

begun, and in this strange vacuum the inhabitants carry on their affairs, meetings and partings, gift-makings and match-makings, with a precision and intentness that magnify and dignify all their performances. It was one of the most perfect settings for satirical comedy that has ever existed; at all other times the writers of such comedy have been faced with the necessity of creating an artificial world in which to work, and even the most brilliant sometimes failed to carry conviction. They robbed their characters of reality in robbing them of those intellectual passions and physical sufferings which have no place in comedy. But Jane Austen had no need to create an artificial world, for the real world had approached sufficiently near to the inane for her purpose. Emma Woodhouse, her most cultured and intelligent as well as her most charming heroine, is without an idea in her head. She can find so little to employ her time or occupy her ingenious brain that she must go out of her way to mismanage the foolish little existences of those about her. She knows so little about the direction and nature of her own feelings that her first realisation that she is in love comes to her negatively, in the memorable scene when " it darted through her with the speed of an arrow that Mr. Knightley must marry no one but herself."

Many parallels and similarities to the conventions and manners and the moral code of the Austen novels may be found in Cowper, particularly in the moderation and delicacy of his attachments. His ignorance of all unruly emotions, which might easily have proved a weakness, was fortified by his promptness in banishing, whatever the sacrifice, any elements that endangered tranquillity and security. His friendship with Lady Austen threatened for a moment to break out into a conflict of jealousy and claims, but Cowper behaved with the scrupulous attention to duty and good manners that marks him as of the same breed and pattern as Mr. Knightley and Fanny Price. It was the golden age of the writers upon conduct and religious education. Dr. Gregory took the place now occupied by Freud or Jung, and even Jane Austen herself, evading her responsibility at the climax of her story, fell back, perhaps with a touch of satire, upon the clap-trap of the *Young Ladies' Companion*. "She spoke then, on being so entreated. What did she say? Just what she ought, of course. A lady always does." Cowper was at no time a satirist, and if his eye and mind had been keen enough to do what Jane Austen's did, he might still have lacked opportunity to keep the one employed and the other nourished, since even within the narrow existence described, he and Mrs. Unwin had built up an inner seclusion and retirement. But as far as Cowper mixed with the country gentry of his day he mixed with types of people whom Jane Austen's novels have made familiar to us. The Unwins and the Woodhouses, the Throckmortons and the Dashwoods belong to the same anomalous social group. They believed in the present with a remarkable steadiness and imperturbability, innocent of the regrets for a past golden age or of the hopes for a future one which have distracted the minds of men and women throughout history. We ourselves, however sceptical of the reality of a golden age, look back wistfully to the past and look forward doubtfully to the future. Cowper not only accepted the present as good on the whole, but was incapable of criticising some of its least perfect parts. While Fitzgerald, in viewing England even as early as 1844, declared that "the law of generation must be repealed," Cowper regarded the steady increase of William Unwin's family as a matter wholly for congratulation.

"Never be afraid of the multiplication of children; you do not make them yourself, and He that does, knows how to provide for them. Poor bare-breeched Billy, to whom your alms were yesterday so acceptable, has no desponding thoughts upon this subject, though he has now four, and considering the age, and the age of his wife, may possibly have fourteen."[1]

Later on, with as little common sense but rather more humour, he comforts William Unwin with the tale of a vicar of Olney who thought he would go mad with two or three children but "thought no more about the matter" and felt perfectly easy when he had a dozen. Perhaps later still dim notions of eugenics may have crossed his thoughts when William wrote asking his advice on the cure of knock-knees and squints, but if so there is no record of it. "Walnut shells," he writes, "skilfully perforated, and bound over the eyes are esteemed a good remedy for squinting."

But it must not be supposed by this that Cowper thought human nature had arrived at perfection. Far

[1] William Cowper to William Unwin, December 24th, 1780.

from it. *The Task* itself was written with a set purpose, "to discountenance the modern enthusiasm after a London life, and to recommend rural ease and leisure, as friendly to the cause of piety and virtue." From the long and serious letter to William Unwin on the subject of face-painting, we know that he thought it very improper as practised by Englishwomen, but not by the French, since with them no deception could be intended, "for they do not, as I am most satisfactorily informed, even attempt an imitation of nature, but besmear themselves hastily, and at a venture, anxious only to lay on enough." But a gulf lies between such comments upon fashionable vices and the attitude of Walpole or Lady Bessborough to the condition and future of the nation; Cowper was untroubled with any historical sense, and was therefore incapable of serious comparison between the times as he knew them and better or worse ages. His dissatisfaction with civilisation could as a rule be traced to his having observed how unlike society ladies were to Mrs. Unwin, and society gentlemen to William or Mr. Throckmorton.

He knew that he possessed a mind seldom at its ease in the consideration of large matters, he had "no more right to the name of a poet, than a maker of mouse-traps has to that of an engineer." His modesty and timidity were excessive, nevertheless he understood himself; it was for Shelley to be a faulty engineer, Cowper's true destiny lay in making the perfect mouse-trap. "But thus it is with my thoughts," he wrote, apologising for one of his charming letters, "when you shake a crab-tree the fruit falls; good for nothing indeed when you have got it, but still the best that is to be expected from a crab-tree."[1] Another time, after burning some poems:

"Alas! what can I do with my wit? I have not enough to do great things with, and these little things are so fugitive, that while a man catches at the subject, he is only filling his hand with smoke. I must do with it as I do with my linnet; I keep him for the most part in a cage, but now and then set open the door, that he may whisk about the room a little, and then shut him up again."[2]

This recalls Mrs. Carlyle's canary, or Mme de Sévigné—"La petite Mousse a une dent de moins, et ma petite-fille une dent de plus: ainsi va le monde." Cowper understood as perfectly as any woman writer how to work in miniature; one of his favourite stories was that of Sam Cox in deep thought by the sea "wondering that such an almost infinite and unwieldy element should produce a sprat." Many of Cowper's traits are those more commonly found in women than in men. He could talk about himself and his person in a way that comes naturally to many women, with an ingenuous pleasure and interest which were redeemed from even an appearance of ostentation by the peculiarly sweet and light humour of his manner. So he describes to Lady Hesketh his baldness and his skill in disguising it. There being "more hair in the world than ever had the honour to belong" to him, he had intermixed his own with just enough found else-

[1] William Cowper to William Unwin, November 26th, 1781.
[2] *Ditto*, February 27th, 1780.

where and finished it all off with a small bag and a black ribbon about the neck. He describes how the Throckmortons, having seen him from a hill at a distance, crossed a great turnip field to reach him: "You see therefore, my dear, that I am in some request." One of his most charming characteristics was his unspoilt appetite for little attentions. Of vanity he had none except that which he assumed to entertain his friends. "The two ladies in the meantime were tête-à-tête in the drawing-room. Their conversation turned principally (as I afterwards learned from Mrs. Unwin) on a most delightful topic, viz., myself." He apologises for his shortcomings with an ingratiating prettiness. "If I was as genteel as I am negligent, I should be the most delightful creature in the universe." (Who without knowing the origin of the quotation would dream of assigning it to a man?)

Swift certainly understood the lives and ways of young women as well as if he were one of them, but he wrote as master; he understood without sharing. Cowper not only understood the minds of the women with whom he consorted but was capable of a Tiresian metamorphosis for their sakes. When he chose lodgings for Lady Hesketh at Olney he conducted the business with a perception of the niceties of feminine comfort that is almost uncanny. He waited for the visit with an impatience that matched his concern for the happiness of the visitor. "Well, the middle of June will not always be a thousand years off," he writes in April, and nearer the day of arrival he speaks of himself as "flushed with the expectation of Lady

Hesketh." On the day itself his spirits "instead of being greatly raised, as I had inadvertently supposed they would be, broke down with me under the pressure of too much joy, and left me flat, or rather melancholy throughout the day to a degree that was mortifying to myself and alarming to her"[1]—a condition of things that Lady Bessborough would have understood. Equally feminine was his feeling about Olney when he came to leave it. He found that even the unhappiness he had suffered there endeared it to him. "I was weary of every object, had long wished for a change, yet could not take leave without a pang at parting."

In the circumstances it is not surprising to find none of the robustness in his humour or his fancy that one finds in Lamb. On the other hand Cowper never over-reaches himself, never shocks, is never silly. He does not write letters in alternate lines of red and black ink, and a reader with no sense of humour might read all Cowper's letters without thinking him a fool. Yet Cowper, just as often as Lamb, was merry to disguise his sadness, but he had neither the vitality nor the imagination for excursions such as Lamb's. Cowper wove humour into his text like a silver thread into a silk cloth, and often the thread is so fine and the execution so perfect that one scarcely sees it, but marvels at the lustre of the piece. There is comparatively little that one can quote from his letters as outstandingly humorous or witty, but a tone of humour comes through, a crispness, an archness. "My dear Friend,—I hurry you into the midst of things at once, which if it be not

[1] William Cowper to William Unwin, July 3rd, 1786.

much in the epistolary style, is acknowledged, however, to be very sublime. Mr. Morley, *videlicet* the grocer. . . ." They want a new tea-urn; as for their present one—" a parson once, as he walked across the parlour, pushed it down with his belly, and it never properly recovered itself." He has been sent " an abundant variety of stationery ware, containing, in particular, a quantity of paper sufficient, well covered with good writing, to immortalise any man."

There is a sort of fastidiousness in his drollery, a strut and an air in his anecdotes which coming from someone so sincerely simple and unpretentious, give complete delight. See how he manages the pomposity of the dialogue between himself and the Clerk of the parish of All-Saints, Northampton, who had come to ask for some verses " in the mortuary style " to annex to his yearly bill of mortality.

"' Mr. Cox, you have several men of genius in your town, why have you not applied to some of them? There is a namesake of yours in particular, Cox the Statuary, who, everybody knows, is a first-rate maker of verses. He surely is the man of all the world for your purpose.'

" ' Alas! Sir, I have heretofore borrowed help from him, but he is a gentleman of so much reading that the people of our town cannot understand him.' "[1]

The advantage of wearing one's humour so lightly is that the more serious thoughts and feelings can be intermingled with the less serious without doing violence to either style or matter. From a pun upon

[1] William Cowper to Lady Hesketh, November 27th, 1787.

sex and sexpence[1] to a discussion of God's purpose in removing the innocent from the world and leaving the wicked, the transition may be a little awkward, but it is easy to pass from Mr. Cox and his mortuary verses to one of Cowper's finest and grimmest observations: "Had we eyes sharp enough, we should see the arrows of Death flying in all directions, and account it a wonder that we and our friends escape them a single day."[2] Whether he talks of death, or the scent of fields in the sun, or the self-deception in regretting childhood, "for infancy itself has its cares," or thanks Lady Hesketh for bounties which he can never repay, his manner, like that of his dream-Milton, is one in which we find "equal sweetness and dignity."

"Oh! you rogue!" he wrote to William Hayley, "what would you give to have such a dream about Milton, as I had about a week since? I dreamed that being in a house in the city, and with much company, looking towards the lower end of the room from the upper end of it, I descried a figure which I immediately knew to be Milton's. He was very gravely, but very neatly attired in the fashion of his day, and had a countenance which filled me with those feelings that an affectionate child has for a beloved father, such, for instance, as Tom has for you. My first thought was wonder, where he could have been concealed so many years; my second, a transport of joy to find him still alive; my third, another transport to find myself in his company; and my fourth, a resolution to accost him. I did so, and

[1] See p. 203.
[2] William Cowper to William Hayley, June 5th, 1792.

he received me with a complacence, in which I saw equal sweetness and dignity. I spoke of his *Paradise Lost*, as every man must, who is worthy to speak of it at all, and told him a long story of the manner in which it affected me, when I first discovered it, being at that time a school-boy. He answered me by a smile and a gentle inclination of his head. He then grasped my hand affectionately, and with a smile that charmed me, said, ' Well, you for your part will do well also '; at last, recollecting his great age (for I understood him to be two hundred years old), I feared that I might fatigue him by much talking, I took my leave, and he took his with an air of the most perfect good breeding. His person, his features, his manner, were all so perfectly characteristic, that I am persuaded an apparition of him could not represent him more completely."[1]

A spirit of peculiar graciousness inhabited Cowper. Few people have been more constant or more sane in their love and friendship, more certain whom they liked, more happy in their choice of companions or more indifferent to scandalmongers. He suffered from long and severe seizures of madness and melancholy, but the head-centre of these seizures was God, not man. Indeed the relationship between Cowper and God makes a striking contrast to the relationship between Cowper and Mrs. Unwin. In the first, surrounded as he was with men and women worshipping God as placidly as sheep crop the turf, he was tossed with uncertainty, longing and anguish, sometimes in an ecstasy of happiness, more often in unspeakable

[1] William Cowper to William Hayley, February 24th, 1793.

wretchedness and fear. In the second, in spite of all the difficulties that might have attended a situation with few virtuous precedents, he seems to have known nothing but peace and happiness and love. A little kindliness or humour in a fellow-being was enough to satisfy him; his friendliness slept light and, once awakened, its skill and sympathy always remained alert; but his shoulders were never easy under the yoke of Christ. The first relationship may be the key to the second. Certainly his preoccupation with religion prevented him from taking his writing too seriously, which considering the fragility of his genius was well for him, since it saved him from the incubus of desire for praise or fear of criticism. "God knows that my mind having been occupied more than twelve years in the contemplation of the most tremendous subjects, the world and its opinion of what I write is become as unimportant to me as the whistling of a bird in a bush."[1] Much earlier, writing to his cousin Mrs. Cowper of our natural anxiety for the after life of those we love, he said:

"For my own part this life is such a momentary thing, and all its interests have so shrunk in my estimation, since by the grace of our Lord Jesus Christ I became attentive to the things of another, that, like a worm in the bud of my friendships and affections, this very thought would eat out the heart of them all, had I a thousand. . . ."[2]

A tragic love affair may either drive a man to take no

[1] William Cowper to the Rev. John Newton, August 6th, 1785.
[2] William Cowper to Mrs. Cowper, September 3rd, 1766.

pleasure in humanity or may so quicken his sympathies that he acquires a special ability for friendship. Moreover, suffering tends to purge the dross from every nature; and the very fact that the sufferer is too preoccupied to care intensely for others may dispose him to find a particular consolation in serving them. Cowper *versus* God, a case which lasted the lifetime of the unfortunate appellant, sometimes so wrought upon him that it deprived him of his senses, but in the intervening lulls it served like an open wound to drain the rebellious elements from his disposition, leaving only a singular purity, modesty and charm.

2. LADY BESSBOROUGH

The progeny of John, 1st Earl Gower were so numerous and so well-connected, that if one tried to unpick their names and lives from the closely woven tapestry of the English aristocracy of the eighteenth century, the whole piece would fall in fragments. Pierrepont, Egerton, Wrottesley, Sackville, Waldegrave, Fox, Holland, Harcourt, Cavendish, Russell, Fitzpatrick, Howard—these are only some of the names in the Gower pedigree. Among so many, among so much distinction, the appearance of another grandchild in 1773 might have been an event of small importance. But the child was a boy of singular beauty, the youngest in a family of eight, of which six were girls, the last child to be born to Granville, 2nd Earl Gower,[1] the fourth child and only son of his third wife, Lady Susan Stewart, herself a woman of remarkable culture and charm. Almost inevitably the attention of the family centred upon little Granville George Leveson Gower. Moreover, he was born with the aura of promise upon him; from his earliest days he excited the expectations of his parents and roused the

[1] Created Marquis of Stafford in 1786.

curiosity and admiration of strangers. He was favoured above his fellows, a child Absalom, endowed, as his mother said thirty years later, " with a pleasing form, with engaging Manners, with an excellent Understanding, in an happy Station of Life, bless'd with Affluence, with a good Constitution. . . ." His sisters adored him and his parents looked upon his education, the forming of his character and the planning of his career, as obligations to the child and to high Heaven which could not be too seriously pondered and performed. Their attitude reminds one constantly of the ancient Hebrews, of Abraham and Sarah with Isaac, of Manoah and his wife with the child Samson, of Elkanah and Hannah with Samuel, of Zacharias and Elizabeth, of Joseph and Mary. In our admiration for the urbanity and cheerfulness of the eighteenth century we are apt to overlook its deep seriousness. The government of England and the stability of the Royal Family were matters of intense importance to a family such as the Leveson Gowers, and to bear and educate a child to take his seat in Parliament had become almost the equivalent of raising up a deliverer for Israel, an object fit for the noblest parents in the land and not lightly undertaken even by them.

The story of the young hero-lord has been preserved in the family correspondence of the forty years between 1781 and 1821, lately edited by Castalia, Countess Granville. When the story opens Granville is setting out for his first school, Mr. Kyte's at Hammersmith, conducted by no meaner person than the Lord Chancellor, and provided with Partridges, Pineapples[1] and Buns for the journey. From Mr. Kyte's he was sent to a private tutor near Wolverhampton, Mr. Woodhouse, afterwards Dean of Lichfield, whither presents of oranges followed him, and letters from his mother filled with descriptions of Mr. Pitt, a fitting model for her son since "his Passions" were "all guided by Reason." Lord Boringdon and Lord Morpeth were among his companions at Mr. Woodhouse's, and to the distress of Lord and Lady Stafford, they showed a greater knack of self-expression than Granville, "owing to their being less indolent" wrote Lady Stafford, expressing herself with all the vigour of which she was capable. "You, tho' you like to receive letters, will not give yourself Time to answer them, you will not employ your mind. You suck your thumbs, chew your Pocket Han. or a bit of Paper, protest you do not know what to say, get up, sit down, fiddle faddle, and will not take the trouble of thinking."[2] But the joint anxiety of the parents about the mind of their son did not prevent the mother from indulging his fancies and caring for his appearance. Oysters, she writes, are to be sent every week to him, and she hopes he has received the Green Pomatum for putting on his hair three times a week, Honey Water, the secret recipe of Lady Caroline Howard, being provided for a hair wash on the alternate nights.

[1] Lady Bessborough some years later happening to comment on the plentiful supply of pineapples from their greenhouses at Twickenham—when pineapples were a guinea apiece in London—was informed by the steward that hers cost her three guineas apiece to grow.

[2] Lady Stafford to Lord Granville, November 4th, 1786. From *The Private Correspondence of Lord Granville Leveson Gower 1781-1821* (John Murray).

In 1789 Granville went up to Christ Church and the wishes of his parents for him become more explicit as he grows more capable of understanding them. He must " possess every Advantage of which the human Mind is capable " and his mother urges him to apply himself particularly to Mathematics and Logic. Now he begins to move about in the world; he travels to Scotland with Lord Boringdon in the summer of 1790 and to Paris to stay with Lady Sutherland in the beginning of 1791.[1] Lady Sutherland wrote enthusiastically to his mother, in the odious jumble of French and English then fashionable. " Pour moi je l'aime à la folie, and si je n'étais pas d'un *certain âge*[2] ce serait une affaire dangereuse, mais comme je suis la *sagesse même*. I am with regard to him in the situation of an old Fairy qui veille sur un jeune and beau Prince, as you read in old legends and fairy tales. I don't know how he likes the French Ladies, but altogether he behaves with great propriety without quizzing anybody, which is an instance of self-denial."[3] But before the end of the visit her idea of him seems to have changed a little; she gives his mother advice. " Talk a great deal to Granville about the Princesse de Hesse, and tell him how invidious it is to talk much to *married Women*, particularly when they have been living so long quietly and without scandal."[4]

At this moment, however, the dangers of the gaming tables were occupying the minds of Lord and Lady

[1] Lady Sutherland had married Granville's stepbrother, Lord Gower, a few years previously. [2] Twenty-six.

[3] Lady Sutherland to Lady Stafford (1791).

[4] *Ditto*, " February something " (1791).

Stafford to the exclusion of other fears. Lady Stafford warns Granville of his father's extreme horror of gambling, and describes her relief that Lord Stafford was absent when some friend from Paris reported Granville as playing "a game like Hazard." "You had better not answer this," she ends, "as your Papa reads all Letters directed to me." Later in the year her distress is great to find that Granville still wishes to play tennis, for his father had been very emphatic upon its undesirability as leading to "gaming, Idleness and bad Company." Presently hints follow about Listlessness and Indolence—she hopes he has procured "the tub" and goes "constantly into the Cold Bath." A very important stage in his education approaches, his travels are under discussion and giving the parents much thought and anxiety. If they benefit him no more than they do many young men, it will break his mother's heart. "How many of them [the young men who travel] lose all Idea of Religion; they hold the Government of the Passions in Contempt, connect themselves with married Women, and return what the World calls a fine Gentleman."

The first chapter of Granville's travels, in Russia Poland and Austria, was brought to a close by a summons from his father to join his regiment (a company of Staffordshire militia) shortly after France had declared war. But six months later we find that he has obtained leave of absence and is on his way to Italy by sea, whither his mother's enchanting tirades follow, warning him now against the "Claws" of an "artful Woman" who might "draw the best disposed into horrible Scrapes." She admitted that she had particular claws in mind, possibly those of Mrs. St. John, to whose influence over him by flattery she refers teasingly in a later letter; or it is just conceivable that knowing Granville must meet the Bessboroughs in Italy she remembered the reputation of Lady Bessborough—Byron's " Lady Blarney "—for the captivation of both old and young.

But Granville seems to have returned from Italy heart-whole, although sufficiently interested in Lady Bessborough to extract a half promise from her (which she fulfilled) to write to him. Her first letters are significantly full of references to her age, to reformation and the attainment of wisdom. " I trust and hope I am grown old and wise enough to be certain of never again involving myself in the misery of feeling more than the common Interest of friendship for any one—je n'ai plus de prétensions, je ne dois plus avoir de préférences."[1] She had to wait for his letters at first; he seems to have accepted her attentions rather casually, considering that she was a woman entirely his equal in rank and intelligence, twelve years his senior and almost as popular a beauty as her sister the Duchess of Devonshire. But by November 1794 (they had met first in February) either Mrs. St. John had palled or he had realised his good fortune, for he complained that she had not written; he had promised her not to gamble and claimed as reward a lock of hair. By January she had cause to tease him about a dreadful conflagration which threatened to consume him. The

[1] Lady Bessborough to Lord Granville, June 1st, 1794.

Spring brought his old tutor Mr. Woodhouse to Trentham, asking Lady Stafford " very obnoxiously " if Granville " had applied a great Deal this Winter."

" Your Mother was a little confounded, for Ladies, late Hours, Cards, House of Commons, sensible companions, dissipated Friends, St. James's Street, The Church, Hyde Park, good intentions, broken vows, repentance, Love, and Operas, all presented themselves (in a single medley) to my mind. I could not—no, you know I could not say that you had hurt your Health by Study or Business. I did not like to say that your Looks or your Morals were in a chancelant Condition, nor did I like to tell him a *thumping Fib*, and make your worthy Friend believe that you were an example to all studious young Men, and a Shame to those who are idle and dissipated. So after staring like a Conjuror, I stammered out a few words expressing that you had not lost much time in study."[1]

In the next eight months the intrigue developed quickly. By January of 1796 Granville was in a position to complain of Lady Bessborough's showing too much favour elsewhere, and she had become sufficiently humble in her attachment to beg that they might not spoil the few moments they had together by wrangles and complaints. In the course of this year Lord Holland eloped with Lady Webster and gave the Staffords a text from which to preach the " Misery, Disgrace and Ruin " that follow, not tennis now, but irregular connections. The moral reflections in Granville's reply gave his father much pleasure. His

[1] Lady Stafford to Lord Granville (1795).

mother was too shrewd to commend—"but *I say* you are a little cunning Villain," she wrote. In the autumn of 1796 we find him in Paris with Lord Malmesbury—his first diplomatic appointment—and writing in his stiff way to Lady Bessborough "My morals are not as yet tainted." She quizzed him upon the diplomatic formality of his style; nothing could be more natural than her letters now. Reserve is banished; she can tell him how she sat up until eleven at Holywell, an hour after the household had gone to bed, listening at the open window to the nightingales and waiting impatiently for the postman, who had to be bribed to tie his letters to a string so that she could haul them up. Now the never wholly attractive figure of Lord Granville, "too fine a gentleman to like ugly people,"[1] begins to take a second place in the story told by the correspondence. Lady Bessborough is too alive for him to survive except as the object, the curious object, of her affections.

What sort of a woman was Lady Bessborough? The contemporary views of her and her sister are contradictory and many. They were everything good, everything bad; honourable, dishonourable, true, faithless, the best of parents and the worst of parents, gluttonous of pleasure, unselfish to a fault. It would be absurd to claim that the evidence for the proper verdict is to be found in the Granville Leveson Gower correspondence; the man or woman has yet to be born who can see all his or her own failings in just proportion, and however

[1] So Lady Caroline Ponsonby, Lady Bessborough's daughter, remarked when she was suffering from chicken-pox as a child.

quick to find fault a lover may be, he is almost certain to take a kinder view of his mistress than the world does. The most reliable testimony to Lady Bessborough's goodness as well as to her charm must lie in the fact that, after years of very natural disfavour, she won over Lord Granville's family. Even Lady Stafford, far too shrewd to be deceived by a show without reality, and very outspoken in her disapproval of the kind of life led at Chatsworth, and the late hours that sent Granville back to London looking pale and languid, even she before many years had passed came to speak of Lady Bessborough with kindness and warmth. In 1803 she wrote to her son:

"This night I received from Lady B. Ly M. W. Montagu's Life and Letters, and she sent with them two Caricatures of Buonaparte, and Mr. Ad., Brother Hily, and Brother Bragge, with Lord Hawkes, in one of them. Her attention and Kindness to me are unceasing. I am really ashamed of the Expense. The Pellisse and the Books are not Trifles, and I do not believe that she is very rich. That she is generous, benevolent, and of a most affectionate Disposition I knew long ago, and I feel her Kindness, and I want you to find out Something that she would like, and would not bestow upon herself (though she would delight in purchasing it for another). I say I want you to find out something that would cost about 10 or 15 Guineas, and give it from me, and I will send you the Money Forthwith. . . ."[1]

In Lady Bessborough as in her sister, natural

[1] Lady Stafford to Lord Granville, June 18th, 1803.

vitality was so great that contradictory elements could war within her all through life without reaching a compromise or suffering extinction. She had the spontaneity and imprudence of a child, embracing life as it came to her, seldom analysing it. As often as not her experiences saddened and revolted her, and yet with such resilience nothing could age her mind or dull her appetite for life. This was her secret; never to undergo the exhaustion of thinking too precisely or the boredom of knowing too much, and she became a grandmother before altogether ceasing to be a girl.

Such naivety did not appeal to all her acquaintances. Byron, for one, was bored and irritated; he showed his underlying sanity and common sense in contact with her, complaining to Lady Melbourne how difficult it was to satisfy the mother of the tiresome Caroline, since Lady Bessborough was divided between fears for the consequences of Caroline's affair and " anger that so interesting a heroine should not be adored in the oldest, and most tedious fashion of feminine worship." Hare once said that she would have made the fortune of her clients as a man and a special pleader, since she had " more shifts and turns and ingenuity in supporting a bad argument than anybody he ever met with." Such furious loyalty to those she loved would have meant self-destruction to anyone not already fire and air, and even she could not escape all its consequences. The ill that was spoken of her and of course repeated to her could not fail to pain, for she was shy and sensitive; she envied the composure of other women, and of Lady Sutherland in particular, " for with great cleverness, beauty, talents, and a thousand amiable qualities, she possesses a command over herself and a propriety of manner and conduct that make me look up to her with respect, envy, and, I own, despair."[1] One gathers that Lord Granville was frequently shocked by what he considered her indelicacy—for instance the scandalous impropriety of canvassing for Mr. Fox. His nervousness over her conversational indiscretions is more easily sympathised with.

" You began blabbing out at Supper last night what I had been telling you just before about the Means made use of to surprise the Boulogne Ships. I hope you have not told anyone of the attempt that is to be made upon the pier at C——. . . ."[2]

In spite of her protest that she never knew how to say the right thing at the right moment she was clearly an excellent talker, with the ready catholic sympathies which provoked confidences of all sorts from a great variety of casual acquaintances, as well as from her particular friends. She did not lack the courage to follow Mme de Staël's advice: " Quand la conversation languit il faut rompre en visière pour la rendre intéressante, il vaux mieux risquer une impertinence que de s'ennuyer." She had a sense of character, particularly in remarkable men. Nelson is " dear delightful Nelson," in her letters, and the stories she collected about Napoleon would together constitute a biographical essay. During her visit to Paris in 1803 she saw him mounted on an old white horse that had

[1] Lady Bessborough to Lord Granville, October 6th, 1795.
[2] Lord Granville to Lady Bessborough, October 5th, 1804.

been Louis XVI's. " What is the line in Richard the 2nd when he asks the groom if Roan Barbary look'd grandly under Bolingbroke: it haunted me all the time," she wrote to Granville. Her favourite reading was books about great men, by great men—Swift's *Journal to Stella*, Boswell's *Johnson*, and after that history. In 1807 she is full of Rulhière's *Histoire de l'Anarchie de Pologne* and begs Granville to read it. Her tastes did not always coincide with Granville's and she hesitated about sending him *The Lay of the Last Minstrel*, although she recommended *Sense and Sensibility* as having amused her very much. Miss Austen might amuse her but a sentimental novel always went straight to her heart. She wept over the Présidente's fate and Valmont's cruel letter in *Les Liaisons Dangereuses*. She wept over *Delphine*. At the theatre she saw Betty, the boy actor, in *Lovers' Vows*, famous now as the ludicrous piece that caused such a to-do in *Mansfield Park*, and cried her eyes out. " The detail of all ye disadvantages a natural child must suffer would alone have affected me," she said, thinking no doubt of " the real Eliza," the Duchess of Devonshire's daughter by Lord Howick, whose fate since the death of the Duchess lay much on Lady Bessborough's heart.

One is struck that such intelligence and knowledge of the world could live side by side with so little real sophistication. But so it happens sometimes. Ellen Terry was of the same quality and it seems clear that Lady Bessborough did not fall far short of Ellen Terry in charm and native allurement. A private note has survived among the correspondence that in several of its particulars might be capped from Ellen Terry's own experience.

" Pour la rareté du fait et la bizarrerie des hommes, I must put down what I dare tell nobody—I should be so much asham'd of it were it not so ridiculous. At this present April, 1812 in my 51st year, I am courted, follow'd, flatter'd and made love to, en toutes les formes, by four men—two of them reckon'd sensible, and one of the two whom I have known half my life—Ld. Hd., Mr. Ward, Young Montagu, and little Matty. Sir J. C. wanted to marry me when I was fifteen, so from that time to this—36 years, a pretty long life—I have heard or spoke that language, and for 17 years of it lov'd almost to Idolatry the only Man from whom I could have wish'd to hear it, the man who has probably lov'd me least of all those who have profess'd to do so—tho' once I thought otherwise."

Much of the gallantry which Lady Bessborough inspired was grossly importunate, mortifying rather than flattering. Curious scenes are described—one between herself and Sheridan and his second wife Hecca, which continued until three in the morning, when the drunken Sheridan seized Lady Bessborough with such violence that she had to call Mrs. Sheridan's maid to help her lock him in before she could make her escape from the house; another at the end of 1809 with the Prince of Wales, " that immense, grotesque figure flouncing about half on the couch, half on the ground," trying to endear himself by giving a list of Granville's inconstancies, sobbing and crying, flinging himself upon her, promising her anything—even to give up Mrs. Fitzherbert—if she would become his mistress.

But it would be difficult to maintain on the evidence of Lady Bessborough's letters alone that the English aristocracy of that period was more frivolous or depraved or engrossed with sex than at any other period. Take her description in January 1802 of the geography of Chatsworth on a winter afternoon, with its chess-playing and reading, literary discussions as serious as those of any undergraduate reading party, Euclid in another room, " my sister shut up with Gurdon," and only that ever mysterious character, the 5th Duke of Devonshire, still in bed, and his son Augustus Clifford asleep in a corner; nothing could be more sober and industrious. In her youth the " eager feel " Lady Bessborough had about politics would keep her awake at night. England was to be studied, to be worked for; patriotism was then a career, not a minor virtue. Lady Bessborough was perfectly awake to faults particularly English—the mismanagement and unpunctuality in public celebrations, the conservatism of the services—and to certain merits. " We are by nature a grumbling Nation, but in times of exigency have always hitherto risen when exertion was really wanted," she wrote in 1807 shortly after the battle of Friedland. She, no less than Granville's parents, believed in her country with an almost religious intensity. The signs that national morality was changing, and the structure of eighteenth-century life decaying, distressed and perplexed her.

"You will see in the Gazette today Ld. Collingwood's and Solana's letters. I like the handsome way of carrying on war, so unlike the illiberal manner in which the French and we have got of late years. I delight in the old Chevaleresque fashion of Courtesy and kindness—giving one's faith and dying rather than forfeit a particle of what was promis'd. War has relaps'd into all the savageness of old times without the bright honour and brilliant courage that us'd to make one overlook its cruelty, and negotiation, as you yourself own, is the art of tricking well, instead of simple good faith and plain dealing. . . ."[1]

A couple of weeks earlier, writing of Nelson's death, she said that she felt almost as much envy as compassion. "Do you know G . . . I think I should like to die so. Think of being mourn'd by a whole Nation, and having my name carried down with gratitude and praise to the latest generation." Fourteen years after the Great War such aspirations are as difficult to assess at their contemporary value as is a play like *Lovers' Vows*. But at the time the sincerity of the interest in politics felt by such persons as Lady Bessborough, and their real passion for the welfare of England, sterilised social life. Without its beliefs and principles and fighting instincts—so curiously mixed with its extravagances and intrigues and childishness—society at the turn of the eighteenth-century would have lacked half its brilliance and half its vitality.

The further one follows the Granville Leveson Gower correspondence down the years, the more one is

[1] Lady Bessborough to Lord Granville, November 28th, 1805.

drawn, at least temporarily, to accept the standards and to share the interests of the writers. The details multiply, and yet increase in significance; everything grows of more consequence than it seemed at first; as the children grow up and marry—Lady Caroline Ponsonby to William Lamb, Lord Duncannon to Lady Maria Fane—one begins to understand the parents' interest in their welfare. The hopeless faithfulness of Lady Bessborough, loving "almost to Idolatry . . . the man who has probably lov'd me least of all who have profess'd to do so," is like the love theme of a Chaucerian poem in all its infinite, minute variations, and like it never palls. Her idol was by no means faithful to her. At the opera Sheridan would persecute her "in every pause of the music" with stories of Granville's treachery, while alongside in one box sat his "love" Lady Sarah Villiers, and opposite her another love, Lady Asgill. But apparently he valued her advice more than he feared her jealousy, and confided most of his affairs to her. There are constant references in her letters to old and new flirts, met at this party or at that and found in high beauty; she could appeal to him to verify a piece of gossip about Harriette Wilson and she speaks in the accents of a confidante of his flirtation with Lady Hester Stanhope, Pitt's niece, who afterwards, from her remarkable establishment on Mount Lebanon anticipated the prestige of Colonel T. E. Lawrence.

The greatly coveted young man, no longer quite so young, was finally won in 1809 by Lady Harriet Cavendish, the daughter of the Duchess of Devonshire and Lady Bessborough's niece. She was talented, but plain. Mr. Ward announced the match thus: "His [Canning's] friend, Lord Granville Leveson, is going to marry Lady Harriet Cavendish. Lady Bessborough resigns, I presume, in favour of her niece. I have not heard what are supposed to be the secret articles of the treaty, but it must be a curious domestic document." In a letter written by Lady Bessborough a year and a half after the marriage, a phrase slips out which suggests that resigning a lover even of fourteen years' standing and to a favourite niece could not be easily or quickly accomplished. "You bid me write, Dearest G., but I will not weary you with repeating how heavily the time goes with me when I know you are quite away. . . . After you left me I walk'd to W. St., lest any one should come to me and see my eyes."[1]

Granville appears to have made a good husband, and his wife adored him. The letters of his early married life draw a sober, pleasant picture; they played chess a good deal—it was a favourite game with Lady Bessborough too—and Granville read Paley's *Evidences* aloud to Harriet and his sister; he did not think that Paley treated the subject " with that confidence in the Truth of his opinions " that he would have expected in an Archdeacon. Lady Bessborough's own life becomes in great part a bedside chronicle, a record of the deaths of her friends and the births of her grandchildren. She addresses Granville from a sick-room where a daughter-in-law has been brought to bed and must be " constantly talk'd to in a calming soporifick

[1] Lady Bessborough to Lord Granville, July 1811.

way." "Oh," she says, "what stories I could tell you of cross births and hard labours! What receipts I could give you for every disorder, particularly those incident to the human frame between one hour old and three Months."[1] Lady Stafford had died while Granville was in Russia; Mr. Pitt had died, and after days of terrible suffering, her beloved sister had died. Then Mr. Fox, always a great friend and favourite, fell dangerously ill. Her letters describing her visit to him on June 29th, 1806, and his death in the following September are among the most moving and convincing that she ever wrote. As we read them, the spoken word of the dying man still seems to tremble on the air.

"... Then turning to me, he said: 'Talking of the handsomest Man in England reminds me of a friend of yours who has good qualities enough not to want his beauty. I hope we shall have him here soon.' He begg'd me to take off my veil. I told him I had better not. Mrs. Fox said: 'I have prepar'd him not to expect to see you look well.' I took it off, and he took my hand again, and with tears in his eyes said: 'Come, come, this must not be. You must remember our Russian friends, who will be startled if they see you look so.' I assured him *truly* that I was well. He answer'd: 'This is a sad world, what with vexation, sorrow and illness, so we had better play at chess.'"

Now she began to feel that she had lived in a "dream of illusions," buoyed up by her "natural good spirits . . . the delightful society I liv'd in, my friends . . . the adulation which for some reason or

[1] Lady Bessborough to Lord Granville, 1812.

other I often met with in the world." But she dreamed no longer, " I see myself in all the follies and weaknesses of youth, on the verge of old age, its infirmities, its desolateness threatening me on every side."[1]

They were years of war too. She travelled night and day from Milan to Brussels when the news of Waterloo came, for her son Frederick Ponsonby was shot in both arms and received three stabs in the body—after which the Prussian cavalry rode over him and he lay all night upon the field. The years from Waterloo until her death are slenderly documented; she did not write so frequently, perhaps not all the letters were preserved, and not all that were have been published. The veil is not lifted from the sad face, except for a moment at the end, in her last letter written nine days before her death from the bedside of " William's beautiful boy," a little grandchild dying, like Marjorie Fleming, of water on the brain.

[1] Lady Bessborough to Lord Granville, May 7th, 1806.

3. MRS. CARLYLE

A peculiar full-heartedness characterised the vitality of the Devonshire House circle. Lady Bessborough accepted life with ardour; whether the occupation of the moment was loo or politics or the lying-in of a daughter, she gave herself to it without reserve, her whole mind dwelt in it. Mrs. Carlyle's vitality was of a very different order; she never gave herself unreservedly to anyone or anything and the sophistication of her mind has probably never been surpassed by that of any woman. With Lady Bessborough, on the other hand, sophistication was purely superficial, the result of living in a world where after a few years' experience "on a toute honte bue."[1] The daughter of a Haddington doctor, educated in the village school, married at twenty-five to an obscure and struggling writer, might be embarrassed to find herself breakfasting with eight men and only one woman; she could not accept life with the ignorant carelessness of a great-granddaughter of the Duke of Marlborough, but in true knowledge of the world Mrs. Carlyle had the advantage over Lady Bessborough. Life was in many

[1] Mme du Deffand to Horace Walpole, May 21st, 1766.

ways deceptively simple for the aristocrats of the eighteenth century; they sat at table eating off silver plate and congratulating themselves upon the profusion of pineapples from their greenhouses, never doubting that they were easy and cheap to grow. In the hands of their own stewards and attendants and servants, they were protected like petted children from the discomfort of knowing anything of domestic economy. Moreover they were protected from one another. With loyal and tactful retainers, in their spacious and numerous houses, marital difficulties were constantly being smoothed over and removed out of sight, and intrigues conducted with the decorum that sanctified them in the eyes of society.

At 5 Cheyne Row after seventeen years of married life, Mr. and Mrs. Carlyle might still have been found trying to write at the same table. Carlyle complained of the squirting of Jane's pen, while Jane confessed that her husband's presence was a shadow between her and her correspondent. Downstairs in the dim kitchen with its pump and its blackbeetles lived Helen or Ann, not in any sense a protector or a resolver of difficulties, but herself one of life's most persistent problems, relieving her mistress of the labour of cleaning and cooking, but laying upon her heavy enough burdens of another sort. Even with the best servant, conduct was an anxiety, health a responsibility and the working of the mind a perpetual enigma. Carlyle on the one hand and Helen or Ann upon the other, form the two chief topics of Mrs. Carlyle's letters apart from herself (an inexhaustible source of good copy). For her the business of life included neither loo nor politics nor the lying-in of daughters, but something far more complicated—the daily adaptation to managing a servant and to living in close proximity with a husband. She was far too highly civilised to undertake either task complacently or easily. She criticised, complained, mocked, expostulated; and her competence to deal with any situation did not lessen its absurdity or its difficulty.

Yet in a curious way her career suited her. She liked to " see something going on and to help its going on "; it fulfilled a want of her nature, she said, and all the household cares—painting, cleaning and building—gave her more satisfaction than she ever admitted. She said once that God intended her to be a detective. Bugs and barking dogs she hunted down with furious ingenuity and energy, posing as a martyr to domesticity but always excited by the combination of pettiness and urgency in her duties. Her head ached but she must be up and out to sell watches for Mazzini, or to sit for her portrait because Gambardella would take no excuse. A childish restlessness and need for entertainment consumed her, and her recoveries from illness and depression were often as sudden and irrational as those of children. She has been ill—the usual sort of attack, a prolonged bad headache, pains in her limbs so bad that she can hardly get up or sit down without screaming, a treatment of blue pills hardly less disagreeable than the disease—but Darwin calls and says that she looks as if " she needed to go to Gunter's and have an ice " and she not only yields to his persuasion but confesses to being considerably revived by driving to Gunter's and having an ice.

In all Mrs. Carlyle's letters her attitude towards things, her interpretation of events, the nature of her reactions, are constantly shaping, altering and re-arranging the facts. Put any other woman into Lady Bessborough's shoes, and she would tell practically the same story, but marry any other woman but Jane Welsh to Thomas Carlyle and the entire drama of life at 5 Cheyne Row would change. The stature of Carlyle as a writer and a prophet has shrunk considerably in the last forty years, but the Carlyle of his wife's letters remains in every way as striking a domestic figure as when she first began to describe him to her cousins and her friends. His whims and antipathies, her own vivid anxiety that his whims should be humoured and his antipathies not awakened, the unforeseen disasters that a piano, a cock, or a careless servant could bring upon them—over and over again this is the theme of her letters. The setting changes little, two of the three protagonists not at all; there is the passive but not silent sufferer, Carlyle; the silent, active deliverer, Mrs. Carlyle; and the Evil One, the time-old tendency of the "adversary" to torment and perplex the innocent, finding his incarnation in a piano or a bug. Yet it is important, dramatically, that we should not sympathise too much with Mr. Carlyle. We must realise that it is his own inadaptability and his marital stupidity which make him often such an easy victim. So Mrs. Carlyle plays the part of the

Fool to his Lear and finds a subtle pleasure in pricking him between the joints of his armour. " Mr. C. was just come in from his ride, very tired, and, to do him justice, very ill-humoured. . . ." Mrs. Carlyle appears to be the first wife to leave on record that she did her husband this sort of justice. His placidity and apathy when anything went wrong with others instead of with himself were, as she fully appreciated, even more vulnerable spots at which to aim. When the dog Nero had jumped out of an upper window into the street, " Mr. C. came down from his bedroom with his chin all over soap and asked, 'has anything happened to Nero ?' 'Oh Sir he *must* have broken *all* his legs, he leapt out at *your* window!' 'God bless me!' said Mr. C. and returned to finish his shaving."[1] On the memorable occasion when a blackbeetle entered the ear of the maid Ann, Mr. C. of course " took it coolly, as he takes most things. 'Syringe' he said: 'syringing will bring out any amount of blackbeetles.' There is an Apothecary at the bottom of our street; I threw a table-cover about her, and told her to run to him; and begged Mr. C. to go with her, as it was a dangerous thing for *me* to go out in the night air. 'Go with her ?' he said. 'What good could it do *my* seeing the beetle taken out of her ear ?' . . ."[2] So in the end Mrs. Carlyle gets her cloak and bonnet and rushes after the girl, barely escaping a cold in consequence.

But there lay a difference between doing Mr. Carlyle justice when writing to her cousin Jeannie

[1] Mrs. Carlyle to Jeannie Welsh, March 25th, 1850.

[2] Mrs. Carlyle to Miss Agnes Howden, November 23rd, 1857.

Welsh or to her old friend Mrs. Russell of Thornhill, and doing him justice in conversation with Samuel Rogers. When Mrs. Carlyle tilted with Rogers, the peculiar small-minded spitefulness of the Regency days, such spitefulness as Sheridan had shown to Lady Bessborough, met its match. Mrs. Carlyle belonged to the new era. She was to a surprising extent the modern woman, intolerant, hardy, self-possessed, sharp as a needle. " Before dinner " (at Charles Dickens' in the spring of 1849) " old Rogers, who ought to have been buried long ago, so old and ill-natured he is grown, said to me pointing to a chair beside him, ' sit down my Dear—I want to ask you; is your husband as much infatuated as ever with Lady Ashburton ?'—' Oh of course ' I said *laughing*, ' why shouldn't he ? '—' Now —do *you* like her—tell me honestly is she kind to *you*—as kind as she is to your husband ? ' ' Why you know it is impossible for *me* to know *how* kind she is to my husband; but I can see she is extremely kind to *me* and I should be stupid and ungrateful if I did *not* like her.' ' Humph! (disappointedly). Well! it is very good of you to like her when she takes away all your husband's company from you—he is always there isn't he ? ' ' Oh good gracious no! (still laughing *admirably*) he writes and reads a good deal in his own study.' ' But he spends all his evenings with her I am told ? ' ' No—not all—for example you see he is *here* this evening.' ' Yes,' he said in a tone of vexation, ' I *see* he is here this evening—and *hear* him too —for he has done nothing but talk across the room since he came in.' Very devilish old man! but he got no satisfaction to his devilishness out of *me*."[1]

The failings, the illusions and the self-deceptions of Helen and Ann, however remote from those of Carlyle, were all as faithfully and carefully preserved in Mrs. Carlyle's museum of human oddness. At times they supplied her with sayings which described succinctly a twist of the mind so sympathetic to her that the words became part of her verbal currency. "There has been *some* mercy shown, for a wonder!" had been Grace McDonald's remark when she had broken her arm but not the glass of her watch, and it expressed precisely the sardonic appreciation Mrs. Carlyle herself felt for many of the acts of Providence. She used the unconscious humour of less perceptive people than herself to make her own conscious humour. While many writers, Walpole for example, Mme du Deffand, Lady Bessborough, repeat only what has been said by those as witty as or wittier than themselves, Mrs. Carlyle scarcely ever repeats anything but foolishness or naivety. Her cleverness lies in always selecting what is just short of the nonsensical and redeeming it from any trace of nonsense by her use of it. For instance, at Lady Cullum's old curiosity shop—"To all which I felt inclined to answer in Helen's favourite phrase of admiration: 'How expensive!'" Similarly phrases and quotations from Mazzini and others were remembered and used chiefly to make her point even finer than would be possible with normal conventional language. By describing

[1] Mrs. Carlyle to Jeannie Welsh, Holy Thursday, 1849.

Geraldine Jewsbury's friendship with Mr. —— as being " for a long time . . . an intimacy ' with the reciprocity all on one side ' " she implied far more than could be said in so small a space.

The knowledge of Scottish dialect gave additional fibre to her style. It supplied her with Scottish words and phrases to supplement her English and with an appreciation of idiomatic subtleties possessed by few but the bi-lingual or bi-dialectal. From Scotland she got her proverb-making manner of talking—" With such uncertain views of the future there is no getting any use of the present "—and also her indifference to punctilios. Like the Scottish peasant who refuses to take even the highest in the land at their own valuation, she was full of sharpness and wisdom and plain speech. Her descriptions often have the picturesque simplicity that one finds among an uncultured people. Lord Ashburton she described after his wife's death as looking " like a child who had lost its nurse in a wood." On the famous occasion when Nero jumped out of the window—" Lying in my bed, I heard thro' the deal partition Elizabeth scream: ' Oh God! oh Nero! ' and rush downstairs like a strong wind out at the street door." But when she talked the language of books the results were often in the worst pedagogic style. " But I have quite miscalculated my distance, and have left no room for my travels' history since. The loss will not be material. Suffice it to say. . . ." Dorothy Osborne's uncle would have commented with a standish.

Even at its best her style is restless by reason of its

perpetual quotations drawn from family stories and the sayings of friends—a trick with the curious and significant double effect of making her communications intimate and often a little obscure, and yet of increasing her expressiveness and adding to her literary resources. In a world full of boring and stupid strangers, the more incomprehensible to others the language of the elect, the more secure they feel, and the secret language strengthens the bonds of the confederacy.

But Mrs. Carlyle's exclusiveness was largely on the surface. She was ardently interested in people and eager to be liked—so eager to be liked and so hurt when she failed to attract, that she assumed an attitude of indifference and exclusiveness in self-protection. She was always ready to pull another ally within the pale. All her enemies were potential friends, and it required little on the part of the enemy to procure a complete change of feeling; often an appreciative word or a humble gesture would be sufficient. She delighted in consoling Carlyle's strange refugee friends. She rescued them from madhouses and nursed them back to sanity, ate with them surreptitious meals of cake and wine-figs, which had to be hidden in the desk when Elizabeth Pepoli came in with inquisitive eyes. But as soon as anyone else ventured to be kind to her protégé the situation changed. Her comments upon both protector and protected became slightly contemptuous. When the Ashursts took up Mazzini, she summed them up as "a good twadly family" and described her old favourite as being toadied, versified, painted, and receiving flowers, money and so much attention that his head was a little turned.

At the bottom of all this fascinating variability and responsiveness lay a quality for which we have no word; it is the natural complement of "temperament." She was the flint of Geraldine Jewsbury's steel; she was in love, perhaps with Mazzini and certainly with Carlyle, even after thirty years of marriage, or she could scarcely have used such crude methods to hurt him. She even resorted to the devices of jealous school-girls; for instance, the general statement with particular application intended—"I never forget kindness, nor, alas! unkindness either!" She emphasised the virtues of others, leaving Carlyle to observe the contrast between their characters and his. "My cousins," she writes from Scotland, "seem to expect and wish me to make a long visit, and I am not at all likely to take to feeling dull nowadays beside people who really care for me, and have true hearts, and plenty of natural sense. Besides I have two invitations to dinner next week! and have made acquaintance with several intelligent people."[1] For a woman like Mrs. Carlyle to be reduced to using weapons so blunt and heavy upon such an easy victim as Carlyle, presupposes a mind thrown out of gear by disappointment and jealousy. Neurosis would account for the intensity of her distorted feelings, but the nature of the distortion was characteristic.

With her disposition she could no more have been incapable of jealousy even in her sanest years than a

[1] Mrs. Carlyle to Mr. Carlyle, June 29th, 1856.

blood horse could be incapable of going lame. But like many clever women of her emotional disposition she found the career of a hostess provided more satisfaction than matrimony or love affairs, or at least that it was a necessary supplement to these. Her jealousy of Lady Ashburton is not caused merely by Carlyle's enjoyment of her society; it is the jealousy of one clever hostess for another, aggravated by the fact that Lady Ashburton possessed so many advantages of wealth and position that Mrs. Carlyle could hardly compete with her. Even in describing her rival's death and funeral a tinge of envy creeps into Mrs. Carlyle's tone—such felicitous, such accomplished dying! (Nevertheless her own death nine years later in a carriage in Hyde Park was even quieter and more dignified.)

"I never heard of so easy a death. She was dressing about four o'clock; felt faint, and called for Dr. Rous (her private Doctor); he told her in answer to her question, 'what is this?' 'you are going to faint, it is nothing; you mustn't mind these faintnesses!' He put his arm round her to support her; she clasped her hands over his other arm, leant her forehead on his shoulder, gave a sigh, and was dead!

"Last Tuesday Mr. C. went to the Grange to be present at her funeral. It was conducted with a kind of royal state; and all the men, who used to compose a sort of *Court* for her, were there *in tears*! I never heard of a gloomier funeral."[1]

The letters are full of embracings, sudden emotions,

[1] Mrs. Carlyle to Mrs. Russell, May 1857.

the return of wanderers and old admirers, revelations of some new attachment or some disillusionment with trusted friends. She was not in a position to despise Geraldine Jewsbury for fickleness or for continually seeking emotional excitement. There were few who could win and keep Mrs. Carlyle's own confidence and favour. Geraldine herself was perpetually being thrown off and taken back again, abused and appreciated by turns, a comfort one day and a pest the next. Her own mother she adored, but she could not live with her. Even her cousin little Jeannie Welsh, her Babbie, fell at last into disfavour. It is curious to compare Mrs. Carlyle's opinion of Babbie's talents before and after the breach. Before it she wrote:

" Babbie of My Affections,

Thanks to thee for thy nice long clever letters; which supply for me the place of John Sterling's powerful telescope—a Babbie that really shines in narration! Everything from Sterling's champagne to Helen's sore leg, is set before me with a most praiseworthy distinctness, and 'not without' (as Carlyle would say) 'a certain shy sarcasm, peculiar to the family.' "[1]

For nine years she wrote thus ardently and constantly. Then Babbie chose to " pitch her tent in this 'valley of the shadow of marriage.' " The sister Helen took Babbie's place for a little, but Helen died in 1855, and apart from a note, much later, thanking Babbie for a miniature of her daughter there seems to

[1] Mrs. Carlyle to Miss Jeannie Welsh, August 18th, 1842.

have been no further communication. To Mrs. Russell Mrs. Carlyle had written in 1854:

"From my cousins I hear very little now. Jeannie in Glasgow never was a good correspondent; I mean, always wrote remarkably bad letters, considering her faculty in some other directions. Now there is a little tone of married woman, and much made of married woman, added to the dullness and long windedness, that irritates me into—silence."[1]

In the art of calling the pot black there is no better exponent than the kettle, and Mrs. Carlyle excelled in detecting in others the daily inconsistencies to which she was herself so prone. She had the eye and the fingers for microscopic work. With unfailing deftness she abstracted from life the apparently insignificant moments and revealed their essential importance and their relationship to the whole. "Carlyle seemed really pleased with his present and letter—repeated several times over with an air of complacency 'poor little Jeannie!' . . ." The air and the exclamation would have escaped almost anyone but Mrs. Carlyle or Jane Austen. Whether Mrs. Carlyle read Miss Austen and learnt from her is one of the tantalising questions of literary tradition that apparently can never be answered. Mr. Collins' well-known advice to Mr. Bennett upon the treatment of Lydia and Wickham is echoed—consciously one might suppose from the italics—in Mrs. Carlyle's comment upon Mrs. Anthony Sterling's madness: "Happily I never liked her much, so that I can bear

[1] Mrs. Carlyle to Mrs. Russell, July 13th, 1854.

her misfortune *like a Christian*."[1] But she frequently outreaches even Jane Austen in the sharpness of her irony. While Jane Austen's mind was always normal and healthy Mrs. Carlyle's was as sensitive as raw flesh, morbidly acute in its perceptions, and her pen often became a weapon. " Harriet Martineau used to say of me with that show of accuracy never accurate, which distinguished her, ' Jane Carlyle has eight influenzas annually; I wonder how she survives it.' " Anything not simple, natural and unrehearsed aroused an immediate nervous revulsion. The epithet " shy-making " had not been thought of in her day, but she needed it. This was one of the clearest tokens of her modernity; contrast her embarrassed amusement at Mazzini's school celebration with the complacent artificiality of Mme de Maintenon's school and Walpole's innocent pleasure as he inspected it. She suffered from an honest bore to a degree pitiful to observe. After a visit from George Darley she declared that she felt as though she had spent the evening under a harrow. Americans in particular became a severe affliction, and when the " tall, lean, red-herring-looking " man intruded upon her at Chelsea, she discarded her usual courteous ways, snubbing him with not less hardihood than he showed in his unwanted friendliness. She could never bring herself to excuse tediousness because it was accompanied by good nature, nor overlook the disadvantages of a gift out of gratitude. An elvish honesty possessed her; she refused to accommodate herself to people or

[1] " You ought certainly to forgive them as a christian, but never to admit them in your sight, or allow their names to be mentioned in your hearing." *Pride and Prejudice*, ch. xv.

things if they did not really please her. The hairbrush which Carlyle gave her " might have been made on purpose for Goliath of Gath " and the cloak, another gift, she described as " a wonderful cloak for *him* to have bought—warm, and not *very* ugly—and a good shape—only entirely unsuitable to the rest of my habiliments." Her attitude to good fortune was all in the tone of her parenthesis when she described a new maid recommended for her ability in cooking fish: " Pity we never eat fish hardly."

Nothing was ever perfectly to her satisfaction; her querulousness fills in the shadows in every episode of her life, making the outlines hard and clear. Both her inferiority and her superiority in the presence of the male she felt vividly. When Tennyson and Moxon paid an unexpected evening visit in Carlyle's absence, she was openly flattered to be treated as if she were a clever man and talked to for three hours, while Tennyson drank brandy and water and " a deluge of tea," and smoked innumerable pipes; she was flattered, but she was exhausted, and confessed to being " strained to a terrible pitch of intellectuality." But on the other hand there were masculine absurdities to be exposed which completely righted the balance in favour of her own sex. She took particular satisfaction in making sport of the enemies' own methods of warfare. " Lady Godiva and patient Grizzel, etc., etc.," she ridiculed as " mere creations of the masculine brain got up for its own diabolical purposes." Her attitude and her expression of it are as a rule so completely emancipated that one is surprised to find that she could be both timid and prudish, and flinch from situations that would have presented no fears at all to Lady Bessborough. Richard Monckton Milnes had invited Mrs. Carlyle and her friend Geraldine Jewsbury to breakfast, because Geraldine, having published *Zoe*, was now a celebrity. "I never made such a comfortless breakfast in my life—the situation would just have suited Lady Harriet, but me it was too *strong* for—obliged to make conversation with all these men brought to meet us—and obliged at the same time to keep an ear open to what Geraldine was saying to her next neighbour lest she should get on dangerous ground. . . . I did not tell her that the chief apprehension which haunted me—was lest I should be mixed up in the minds of these men with *the Chapel scene* and certain other questionabilities in *Zoe*."[1]

These contradictions are curious, but progress is never unqualified in any century. The freedom of speech upon sexual matters which characterised the aristocracy of the eighteenth century was replaced in the nineteenth by a bourgeois reticence; yet at the same time the position of women improved so much that far more than liberty of speech was coming within their grasp. The reaction to the libertinism of the Regency moved quickly. Morality had become fashionable and the next step in social reform, morality qualified by common sense, was not far off. In Mrs. Carlyle there are certain indications that an age which would put common sense before conventional morality was dawning. She expressed a strong prejudice against

[1] Mrs. Carlyle to Helen Welsh, June 18th, 1847.

unmarried women who find themselves pregnant; "It indicates such stupidity," she said. Nevertheless she was full of romance and tenderness and "the poor woman in the concrete, covered with crimson and tears," went to her heart like a knife. When she read *Vittoria Accoramboni* she said it almost made her weep that she was not born two centuries earlier to be the mistress of Bracciano. In her garden at 5 Cheyne Row she tried to grow a nettle she had brought from Crawford Churchyard, her mother's burial place, and when she herself died she left instructions that two candles which she had kept secretly for twenty-four years should be burnt. In their early days of poverty in London, Mrs. Carlyle's mother had bought extra candles to brighten the dining-room for a party. Jane, annoyed by the extravagance and afraid of its giving a false impression, had snatched them from the table and carried them away, to cherish all her days remorse for the pain she caused and to plan this ghostly and morbid celebration as an atonement. She was full of superstition too. When Lord Ashburton brought her some "things" from his dead wife's wardrobe they "shivered her all through" and the sight of a coffin in the street shortly afterwards made her so nervous that she had difficulty in restraining herself from screaming. Sir James Crichton-Browne attributes the craving for horrors which grew so marked in her later life to "cerebral neurasthenia," but her Scottish superstition and an innate love of anything sensational had given her a bent towards the horrible long before her mental state became disorganised.

Looking back over the two centuries in England and France that preceded these letters one must admit that other women have been as wise as Mrs. Carlyle or wiser, as honest or more honest, as clever, as sensitive, as ruthless. Yet she is unique; one sees in her a fusion of qualities and a quickening of powers unimaginable in any earlier age. It would be hard to discover the equal of Dorothy Osborne or of Mrs. Carlyle in any century, but we know that while we might find another Dorothy in the nineteenth century, we could never find a Mrs. Carlyle in the seventeenth. Life, as embodied in the mind and character of Mrs. Carlyle, had attained an almost freakish complexity and intensity. Just as prehistorically the time arrived when certain four-footed creatures became two-footed and acquired an ascendancy over those which remained four-footed, so a similar evolutionary change has taken place in the last few centuries within the ranks of the two-footed. It may well be that Dorothy Osborne was more lovable than Mrs. Carlyle; but Mrs. Carlyle must be recognised as the superior of the two in her adaptation to an altogether more complicated type of existence. The tendency of social development since the seventeenth century has increased the demand for cleverness and mobility of thought and feeling, qualities which in nine cases out of ten can be fostered only at the expense of charm and depth of character. The modern world, presented with the choice between breeding Dorothy Osborne and breeding Mrs. Carlyle, chooses Mrs. Carlyle.

V

1. SWIFT
2. LAMB

V

1. SWIFT

In himself Swift is unquestionably the most masculine of all the writers in this book and yet his letters to Esther Johnson surpass those of Mme de Sévigné and Mrs. Carlyle in domesticity, and those of every letter-writer in familiarity of language. We get closer to Swift than to Mme de Sévigné; there is a parade of living in her letters; the very bones of living in his *Journal*. Swift could reproduce in his writing not only the spoken word, but the whispered word; his imagination brought his correspondents so close to him that as he wrote he caught himself pursing up his lips into the shape appropriate to the babbling mispronunciations by which alone he could carry on the more affectionate part of his intercourse with Stella and Dingley. By an ingenious system of cross-references he could conjure up for them the actual intonations that his voice would have adopted were he speaking instead of writing.

"I dined to-day"—October 20th, 1710—"with Patty Rolt at my cousin Leach's, with a pox, in the city: he is a printer, and prints the Postman, oh oh, and is my cousin, God knows how, and he married

Mrs. Baby Aires[1] of Leicester; and my cousin Thompson was with us; and my cousin Leach offers to bring me acquainted with the author of the Postman, and says, he does not doubt but the gentleman will be glad of my acquaintance, and that he is a very ingenious man, and a great scholar, and has been beyond the sea. But I was modest, and said, may be the gentleman was shy, and not fond of new acquaintance; and so put it off: and I wish you could hear me repeating all I have said of this in its proper tone, just as I am writing it. It is all with the same cadence with oh hoo, or as when little girls say, I have got an apple, miss, and I won't give you some."

Nothing could be more disconcerting for a reader of Swift previously familiar only with the *Tale of a Tub*, *Gulliver*, the *Modest Proposal*, aware of Swift's arrogance, his ambition, his revengefulness, his sternness, his intolerance of injustice and fraud, his independence, his coldness, to come unwarned upon the *Journal to Stella* and read of deelest lives and logues, sollahs, saucy dallars, Ppts, tonvelsasens—all the jargon of a doating tenderness and what he himself called " a high vein of silliness." But no doubt to a person serious and proud like Swift, to clothe affection in absurdity gave a sense of protection and concealment. He could be frank about an attachment if he could be nonsensical, and the more extravagant and foolish the language of his love, the safer and more secret his real weakness seemed to be. When Swift's

[1] " Aires " is entered as a proper name in the index of Mr. Frederick Rylands' edition of the *Journal* published by Messrs. Bell and Sons.

pen broke off from lucid English into MD, Ppts, Pdfr and Nite poo dee deelests, he was a cunning bird feigning a broken wing to distract attention from the hidden nest. We must remember too that he had first known Esther Johnson when she was a child, brought up in a family bereaved of all its own children, and since she was delicate and charming, no doubt a petted child. Lady Giffard in her character of her brother Sir William Temple says that he was fond of the "imperfect language & natural & innocent way of talkeing" of children, and some of the little Esther's mispronunciations may have passed into family use, to be preserved for years by Swift, Esther and Dingley,[1] that odd little group in Dublin, a fragment broken off from the dignified patriarchal establishment at Moor Park. A household that contained Dorothy Osborne must have been well supplied with the little sayings and phrases that make up family humour, and Swift's *Journal* is sprinkled with oddments of speech that suggest such an inheritance from Moor Park. "You must know I hate pain, as the old woman said," is very much in Dorothy's manner. "Never saw the like," "never was before," "as hope saved," "I don't like it, as the man said." And while we are considering Swift's style and language in the *Journal*, so much nearer our modern English in vocabulary and phrasing than Dorothy Osborne's, only sixty years earlier, mention must be made of his fondness for short,

[1] Rebecca Dingley was, like Swift, a poor relation to whom Sir William Temple had extended his protection and charity. She was one of nine orphans of a cousin who had married on £80 a year.

descriptive words with a savour of the stables about them. He speaks of having "sossed" his hurt leg in a coach. He predicted that when Dillon Ashe went to Bath his face would "whiz in the water"; "scrub" (meaning low-down), "whiffling" (fickle), "wherret" (to vex), "mizzled" (drizzled mist), were other favourites; and "It vexed me to the pluck" (the vitals). Notwithstanding the little language the whole style of the *Journal* is of a piece with such brusque masculine terms. Misspent or superfluous words there are none, nor any words put in to make for easiness of reading. There was never anything further removed from fine writing than the *Journal to Stella*; a style of grunts and curses manifestly shaped for the use of a tough, crabbed nature in an unfriendly world. As he economised his sheets of paper, covering them from top to bottom, from verge to verge, with his close, neat hand, so he economised language, packing half a dozen events and a busy day into three or four lines. And the more he economised the more forceful his style became. "The pain has left my shoulder, and crept to my neck and collar-bone. . . . Urge, urge, urge; dogs gnawing." Particularly one notices it whenever his anger is aroused, and he spits out words and venom; "I will see them rot before they shall serve me so." "So now I am easy, and they may hang themselves for a parcel of insolent ungrateful rascals." "Rot 'em for ungrateful dogs." The frequent virulence of his feelings and of his expression is one of the things that saves his letters from the monotony that might infect a packed record of similar events.

There are some people so endued with individuality and vigour that one can watch them repeating all the small, half-mechanical motions of ordinary life with interest and pleasure. Swift is like that; he makes the commonest particulars of his life in London from 1710 to 1713 fascinating; one apprehends the ferocity and strength of the tiger although one sees him merely grooming himself or crouching to drink.

The relationship between the correspondents suited Swift's mind and temperament to perfection. In London between 1710 and 1713 Swift was a great man, the confidant of Harley and St. John, the peace-maker when they disagreed, the one man to gain favours from them for others (although he could gain none for himself), benefactor to many, without money himself but a patron by proxy, his influence humbly solicited by distinguished persons, hated and feared by the Whigs, courted by all the finest and wittiest young women of breeding and fashion. That this Dr. Swift should seldom rise in the morning or go to bed at night without unfolding all his doings, his plans, his thoughts, his vexations, his bodily afflictions, what he ate, drank, what he spent, so unwillingly, on coach and chair hire, what reception his latest article or pamphlet had received, everything, in fact, to two brats of girls living a life of genteel clerical seclusion, in a Trollope world, was just the situation to charm him. There was something bizarre in it, that he who gave himself so sparingly to his great friends should give himself so freely to Mrs. Esther Johnson and Mrs. Rebecca Dingley at Mr. Curry's house over against the Ram in

Capel Street, Dublin. He teased them on the subject of those secret favours and made out that they gained them solely through impudence and importunity. He said that he did not dare to call them " naughty girls " without inserting " dear," for " O, faith, you govern me." When the affections are involved it becomes an enchanting joke for the master to pose as the creature; the beast delights in roaring like a sucking dove whenever his domination is a certainty.

How Swift could be idle in London between 1710 and 1713 is a riddle, but idle he was; he spent the morning in china shops or book shops (considering his means he was extravagant over books), the evening losing his money at ombre or picquet. In Chelsea—he had lodgings in Church Street near the river for May and June of 1711—he lived like an undergraduate. He used to walk home at the end of the day by Pall Mall and the Park and out at Buckingham House, and observed that in May the hay in the fields between London and Chelsea smelt very sweet, but the hay-makers were not like country girls—" nothing so clean and pretty." The walk made him sleepy in the morning: Patrick came five or six times to wake him. " I tell him I sat up late, or slept ill in the night, and often it is a lie." In the hot May of 1711 he wandered down to the river in his nightgown and slippers and wondered whether he would go for a swim. In June he did swim and the Thames was " pure and warm " but the great stones in the bed of it very sharp to the feet. The " two hundred chapters of madness " which Swift shared with Vanessa belong here, and out of this soil sprang Swift's " pure bites," his anonymous account of Prior's journey to Paris which was " a formal grave lie, from the beginning to the end." Prior showed it to Swift saying " Here is our English liberty," whereupon Swift feigning ignorance read some of it and admired and praised it. Out of this soil also came the note from Swift to Sir Andrew Fountaine which was preserved by Vanessa.

" All that may be; but I stayd yesterday at home for you till two, and if I ever trust to your appointments again, may I stay till two and twenty. . . . As to breakfasting, I will infallibly breakfast with you this morning, and come exactly at ten. To morrow we will tantony[1] as you say, and I will wait for you infallibly till you come. We will drink our Punch on Friday exactly at four without fail.

" P.S. Pray get all things ready for breakfast. Have the coffee, tea and chocolate cut and dry in so many pots, for I will most infallibly come this morning, and very early. The scoundrel you sent is gone to Bloomsbury, so that I fear I shall be with you before my letter. If I do, pray let me know it by a line. And be so kind to burn this before you read it. I am in such hast I have not time to correct the style or adjust the periods; and I blush to expose myself before so great a critick. You know I write without the assistance of books, and my man can witness that I began and finisht this in three quarters of an hour. Knowing that your man will infallibly come back for this letter, I have sent it by Patrick, who is not yet returned.

[1] Possibly meaning " eat pork."

Pray dispatch him as soon as you can, that when your man comes back Patrick may know of him whether he will call or no."[1]

Amongst letter-writers, few besides Swift and Lamb have had the taste and the gift for this sort of humour, and in Swift's case the conditions of his life make his capacity for fooling all the more remarkable. From 1710 to 1713 he was fretting in daily expectation of advancement. As a young man Sir William Temple had disappointed him, after Temple's death William III had disappointed him, after William's death the Whigs had disappointed him. Now the Tories were in and he was their voice to the public, their satirist against the Whigs, their army and their ammunition combined; " Rot 'em for ungrateful dogs " if they did not reward him with a bishopric. As well as a series of tender and humorous love letters, the *Journal to Stella* is a drama of ambition which the reader follows with extreme curiosity and attention. Swift does not tell everything, partly because even before Stella and Dingley he had some pride, partly because it might have been dangerous, but enough comes out to make his hopes and his methods clear. In fact, at times, Swift found it useful to have a couple of female spies in Dublin. He did the Archbishop a good turn, prevented a scandal from being printed, and it was important to know if this altered the Archbishop's attitude towards him. " I will let him know it by next post; and pray, if you pick it out, let me know, and whether he is

[1] Swift to Sir Andrew Fountaine, November 7th, 1711.

thankful for it; but say nothing."[1] We know that Harley, early in the drama (February 1711), sent Swift £50 by a third hand and that Swift refused it and cut Harley for a week, "disliking both the thing and the manner." Harley was tipping him for personal services and Swift looked for an honorarium from the Government; he did not like the "thing" because it was £50 instead of £1,000, just as he despised the deanery of St. Patrick's with which he was finally rewarded because it was not the Bishopric of Hereford. But there was also another reason why he hated his deanery—it meant leaving England and retiring from politics, relinquishing all his power, withdrawing his good services. "I confess," he wrote touchingly to Stella, "I thought the ministry would not let me go." He would rather have been a man of the world than a scholar and the life of London fascinated him. One can see it in his enjoyment of the company of the epicure Charles Dartiquenave (or Darteneuf).

"Darteneuf invited me to dinner to-day. Don't you know Darteneuf? That's the man that knows everything, and that everybody knows; and that knows where a knot of rabble are going on a holiday, and when they were there last."[2]

To the potential author of *Gulliver's Travels* this sort of knowledge appealed far more than the erudition of books, and living in London gave him unique opportunities to acquire it. "So I took up with Mrs.

[1] *Journal to Stella*, April 8th, 1711.
[2] *Ibid.*, March 22nd, 1710-11.

Van, and dined with her and her damned landlady, who, I believe, by her eyebrows, is a bawd."[1]

Swift's grim charities and his meannesses have always excited comment. All his friends knew that he had a curious and careful mind about money (when Addison and Sam Dopping wished to make sure that Swift would receive them they sent up the message that "a gentleman was below in a coach who had a bill to pay"), but like so many who have taken care of the pence, he found the pounds took care to elude him. However, a little speculation that he carried through while in London turned out well; he knew how to manage money, although not how to attract it. When one considers the importance of his articles in *The Examiner*, the huge circulation of any pamphlet written or reputed to be written by him, and the mass of work he did in those three years, it seems to the modern mind almost incredible that from first to last he did not get a farthing in direct remuneration. It was power and position that Swift loved and he wanted money only because it was the most malleable form of power; in his bold refusal of small rewards he probably felt that he made his intention all the clearer and his success more sure. But human nature, and particularly human nature turned politician, is slow to realise obligations that have taken time to mature. Swift had been too proud to take the first tentative gifts; he had made the fatal mistake of never allowing Harley and St. John to form the habit of giving to him.

His sensitiveness was often lacerated while he

[1] *Journal to Stella*, September 14th, 1711.

waited,[1] and his enemies did not lack entertainment. They commiserated with him upon the dilatoriness of his great friends, or, even more humiliating, congratulated him upon appointments that had not been made. Swift's resentment extended even to Stella when she was so rash as to believe gossip and " talk as glibly of a thing as if it were done," which Swift knew was " farther from being done than ever "; he sealed up her offending letter as soon as he had glanced through it, not to be opened for at least a year. It is said that Lord Orrery found a letter of his own to Swift lying in Swift's library several years after it had been written, still unopened. Swift had written on the outside " This will keep cold."

All the malevolence of society in the first half of the eighteenth century comes out as clearly in the *Journal to Stella* as it does in Lord Hervey's *Memoirs*.

" You will think it affectation," wrote Swift in November 1711, " but nothing has vexed me more for some months past, than people I never saw pretending to be acquainted with me, and yet speaking ill of me too ; at least some of them. An old crooked

[1] " O faith, I should be glad to be in the same kingdom with M.D., however, although you were at Wexford. But I am kept here by a most capricious fate, which I would break through, if I could do it with decency or honour.—To return without some mark of distinction, would look extremely little : and I would likewise gladly be somewhat richer than I am. I will say no more, but beg you to be easy, till Fortune take her course, and to believe that MD's felicity is the great end I aim at in my pursuits. And so let us talk no more on this subject, which makes me melancholy, and that I would fain divert. Believe me, no man breathing at present has less share of happiness in life than I : I do not say I am unhappy at all, but that everything here is tasteless to me for want of being as I would be. And so a short sigh, and no more of this." *Journal to Stella*, May 23rd, 1711.

Scotch countess, whom I never heard of in my life, told the Duchess of Hamilton t'other day, that I often visited her. People of worth never do that; so that a man only gets the scandal of having scurvy acquaintance. Three ladies were railing against me some time ago, and said they were very well acquainted with me; two of which I had never heard of; and the third I had only seen when I happened to visit. A man who has once seen me in a coffee house will ask me how I do, when he sees me talking at court with a minister of state; who is sure to ask me, how I came acquainted with that scoundrel."[1]

If an undesirable old acquaintance accosted him, Swift adopted a manner of most chilling civility and vagueness. "I have many friends, and many enemies; and the last are more constant in their nature." It is hardly surprising; Swift encouraged constancy in his enemies and did not always encourage it in his friends. To as much egotism as either Boswell or Pepys possessed, he added an arrogance peculiarly his own. He trained Patrick, his manservant—who drank and read Congreve and bought a linnet for Dingley and is altogether as immortal as any of Mrs. Carlyle's maids—to be admirable at lies and excuses to those who came to beg or waste his time.

"Dr. Raymond called often, and I was denied; and at last when I was weary, I let him come up, and asked him, without consequence, How Patrick denied me, and whether he had the art of it? So by this means he shall be used to have me denied to him, otherwise

[1] *Journal to Stella*, November 22nd, 1711.

he would be a plaguy trouble and hindrance to me: he has sat with me two hours, and drank a pint of ale cost me five pence, and smoked his pipe, and it is now past eleven that he is just gone."[1]

Swift carried out his intentions so successfully that Raymond in a month succeeded in visiting him only four times and while he was dressing, but when the doctor came to take his leave, Swift confessed to a weakness for him very much as a Sultan might confess to a weakness for some tamed creature about his palace. " I was a little melancholy to part with him. . . . He was so easy and manageable, that I almost repent I suffered him to see me so seldom. But he is gone, and will save Patrick some lies in a week. . . ."[2]

There is something pathetic about the store that Swift set upon people who depended on him or gave in to him. He " struck up a mighty friendship " with Lady Kerry and found she had better sense than any other Irishwoman. She was " egregiously ugly " and not at all young, " but perfectly well bred, and governable as I please." One can see how his affection for Harley was increased by Harley's confession that uttering his mind to Swift eased him. The destitute young women whose lot in those days was so wretched, Patty Rolt chased from one cheap country lodging to another, Mrs. Long hiding in King's Lynn from her creditors, could rely on kindliness and even occasional charity from Swift (a guinea sent to Patty Rolt had " patched up twenty circumstances "), for pity and the

[1] *Journal to Stella*, November 25th, 1710.
[2] *Ibid.*, December 20th, 1710.

love of power are often closely connected. But where there is love of power there is also love of revenge. Swift's revengefulness took cold and deliberate decisions. " I owe the dog a spite," he said of Lord Chief Justice Parker, " and will pay him in two months at farthest if I can." Nothing could be more frankly pagan, yet side by side with such remarks we find the evidence of full consciousness of his profession and its obligations. He would go and read prayers to his sick friend Sir Andrew Fountaine and he gave " no man liberty to swear or talk bawdy " in his presence.

Behind Swift's imagining what Stella and Dingley were doing, guessing the very cards they held at ombre and the amount of money they lost, lies the wish to make them feel that he is omnipotent as well as omniscient, and that they are mere puppets, jigging through their days responsive to his twitching of the strings.

" If I was with you, I'd make you walk: I would walk behind or before you, and you should have masks on, and be tucked up like anything: and Stella is naturally a stout walker, and carries herself firm: methinks I see her strut, and step clever over a kennel: and Dingley would do well enough if her petticoats were pinned up: but she is so embroiled, and so fearful, and then Stella scolds, and Dingley stumbles, and is so daggled."[1]

It would be clever enough, if Swift stopped there; but he goes further. He has a way of spiriting Stella from Dublin to his bedside, teasing and being teased, making her an April fool, scolding, yielding to her

[1] *Journal to Stella,* November 10th, 1711.

imagined wheedling, arguing about the right way to spell " business " and trying it six ways himself. Or he is in London and Dublin at the same moment. " I dined with my neighbour Vanhomrigh, and MD, poor MD at home on a loin of mutton, and half a pint of wine, and the mutton was raw, poor Stella could not eat, poor dear rogue, and Dingley was so vexed: but we'll dine at Stoyte's to-morrow."[1]

Swift's ambition and his love for Stella are the cross-currents of the *Journal*. He is ambitious for Stella, to be richer and be able to share his greater comfort with her. (He already gave her an allowance out of his small income.) And yet ambition, by separating them, had become their mutual enemy. " There is peace and quiet with MD, and nowhere else," he says, and for three years he never ceased to promise her and Dingley a near reunion and to comfort himself with the thought of it.

Stella and Dingley must have grown weary and incredulous as the months and years passed and he still promised to return to Ireland and still failed to come. " There is now but one business the ministry wants me for, and when that is done, I will take my leave of them " he had written in August 1711, but before that business was finished another had replaced it, and so it went on. Sometimes, evidently, Stella ventured to rally him a little for his broken promises, more often she seems to have shamed him by her patience. She disguised her disappointment, insisted indeed that it would be wrong to return to Ireland yet. I do not find

[1] *Journal to Stella*, April 4th, 1711.

in the *Journal* the increasing coldness towards Stella and Dingley that Sir Walter Scott mentions.[1] In the last year his letters were interrupted by illness, and for a time were much shorter. After his reply of August 7th, 1712, to the " glib " letter which had upset him so much, nearly six weeks passed before he wrote again, but his explanation can be easily understood and credited:

" I never was so long without writing to MD as now, since I left them, nor ever will again while I am able to write. I have expected from one week to another that something would be done in my own affairs; but nothing at all is, nor I don't know when anything will, or whether, ever at all, so slow are people at doing favours."[2]

The tone of the letters during the summer of 1712 and the winter of 1712-13 is one rather of tired hopes than of tired affection, of depression rather than of disloyalty. Misunderstandings were increasing between his two idols, Harley and St. John, and disaster was threatening the Government which he had helped to build up with so much pride and enthusiasm. William Harrison, the young writer for whom Swift had a particular care and fondness—" the little brat,

[1] See *Works of Swift*, edited by Sir Walter Scott, Vol. I, p. 227: " The effect of his increasing intimacy with the fascinating Vanessa may be plainly traced in the *Journal to Stella*, which, in the course of its progress, becomes more and more cold and indifferent—breathes fewer of those aspirations after the quiet felicity of a life devoted to MD and the willows of Laracor, uses less frequently the affectionate jargon, called the ' little language,' in which his fondness at first displays itself,—and, in short, exhibits all the symptoms of waning affection."

[2] In the same letter (September 1712) occurs a remarkable phrase: " If I had not a spirit naturally cheerful, I should be very much disconcerted at a thousand things."

my own creature"—returned from Holland (where Swift had got him the appointment of secretary to Lord Roby, English Ambassador at the Hague), contracted a fever and died in a few days, to Swift's great grief; and this only shortly after the Duke of Hamilton's death and that of Lady Ashburnham, always a special favourite of Swift's. On the occasion of her death he made one of the very few direct comments upon life that occur in the *Journal*: "I hate life when I think it exposed to such accidents; and to see so many thousand wretches burdening the earth, while such as her die, makes me think God did never intend life for a blessing."

Vanessa may have had something to do with the change of tone in the later letters to Stella, but there is plenty to account for a change without laying it at Vanessa's door. What we miss in them is playfulness rather than affection; there are few of those charming passages in which Swift imagines Stella and Dingley roasting oranges and playing ombre with the Dean and Mrs. Stoyte or pictures them drinking the waters at Wexford—"Poor Dingley never saw such a place in her life; sent all over the town for a little parsley to a boiled chicken, and it was not to be had: the butter is stark naught, except an old Englishwoman's: and it is such a favour to get a pound from her now and then."[1] Dingley evidently had a querulous tone when domestic matters oppressed her. Few now are the occasions when he brings them to his bedside in the morning. For such playfulness the heart must be light as well as

[1] *Journal to Stella*, July 24th, 1711.

fond. But the Swift that wrote " Pray write me a good-humoured letter immediately, let it be ever so short," when he announced that the warrant was signed that made him Dean of St. Patrick's, still looked upon Stella as the " truest, most virtuous and valuable friend " that perhaps anyone ever possessed.

At the same time he knew himself somehow in the wrong—references to the Vanhomrighs show a guardedness from the very first, and Stella very quickly jumped to the conclusion that he favoured them more than he confessed, if one can read her comments between the lines of Swift's replies. With the clumsiness of a genius who prided himself on his worldly wisdom, he did not avail himself of the kind of frankness that might have set her at ease. He said that he dined with his neighbour Mrs. Vanhomrigh because it was raining (she lodged near), because his best gown and periwig had not returned from Windsor; because they laid a trap for him; to save his grazed shin, or " out of mere listlessness." A dozen or more such little excuses where no excuse was asked would have given him away to any woman, and not only to a woman so shrewd as Stella. He described all his young ladies to her but not Mrs. Van's daughters, whom he never even mentioned by name. Clearly Swift felt that the friendship with Vanessa would cause Stella pain and must be hidden from her; no doubt it caused her pain chiefly or wholly because it was hidden from her and therefore made her think that Swift lacked confidence in her generosity and sympathy. It is perfectly clear from the Swift and Vanessa letters that

Vanessa never threatened to replace Stella in his life, but the ideal of monogamy which haunts friends and lovers just as frequently as married people, made him feel that since he loved Stella so much it would be false to love any other woman at all. Moreover, if Stella had known the facts she might have advised him, and Swift possibly feared the soundness of that judgment which he admired so greatly.

The whole business of Swift and Vanessa is a tragedy of " mere listlessness " and lack of foresight. Swift does not seem to have seduced Vanessa or had any intention to seduce her. Horace Walpole, reading one of the references to " coffee " in a letter of Swift's to Vanessa assumed that Vanessa had been his mistress. But if one selects all the references to coffee in all the surviving letters of Swift to Vanessa, while it is evident that " coffee " is a symbol, it is equally clear that it symbolises something less definite and compromising than Walpole supposed. On June 1st, 1722, the Dean wrote to the repining girl, " It would have been infinitely better once a week to have met Kendall, and so forth, where one might pass three or four hours in drinking coffee in the morning, or dining tête-à-tête, and drinking coffee again till seven." Kendall appears to have been a mutual friend, and in any case such a time-table planned for a dean of fifty-five and a young woman more than twenty years his junior suggests friendly rather than illicit intercourse.

But in most of Swift's friendships with women, and young women particularly, he seems to have adopted an attitude of imperiousness and familiarity which is half-way to dalliance. With Vanessa, presumably, her encouragement and their proximity made it impossible to stop half-way, and for more than twelve years the relationship between them had the intensity and the separation from normal life characteristic of a liaison. When Swift in one of his lenient moments wrote in 1720 suggesting a poem commemorating their friendship, his list of the events to be retold is not only incomprehensible now, but would probably always have been so to anyone but himself and Vanessa. Twelve years of secret history and the desire to remember that history and gloat over it together—technical innocence in such circumstances is a bagatelle.

"It ought," Swift wrote of the poem, "to be an exact chronicle of twelve years, from the time of spilling the coffee to drinking of coffee, from Dunstable to Dublin, with every single passage since. There would be the chapter of the blister; the chapter of Madam going to Kensington; the chapter of the Colonel's going to Franc[e]; the chapter of the wedding, with the adventure of the lost key; of the strain; of the joyful return; two hundred chapters of madness; the chapter of long walks; the Berkshire surprise; fifty chapters of little times; the chapter of Chelsea; the chapter of swallow, and cluster; a hundred whole books of myself and so low; the chapter of hide and whisper; the chapter of Who made it so? My sister's money."[1]

But the Swift and Vanessa correspondence, although

[1] Swift to Esther Vanhomrigh, August 12th, 1720.

curious and moving, is only a fragment which the reader of the *Journal to Stella* feels that he must read, just as a man after buying a picture is not satisfied until he takes it out of its frame to see what the frame may hide. In the *Journal* Swift is entire. It even contains, in its occasional vulgarities, a premonition of his most grotesque verses. With Stella and Dingley he could be so sure of appreciation that his description of his life and his feelings—fondness for Vanessa only omitted—has the sort of simplicity and absence of shame that almost no letter-writers achieve, and no diarists but Pepys and Boswell. Stella had accepted Swift as fully as a man accepts himself, and nothing that failed to shock Swift in his own life could shock her.

2. LAMB

When Carlyle accused Lamb of a " ghastly make-believe of humour," he proved nothing except that the Carlyles preferred the humour that consists in seeing one type of reality in opposition to another type. Mrs. Carlyle was a clever and humorous woman, but she never abandoned herself to fooling with her friends; in fact her humour was a variation of her seriousness. The same or similar events at times filled her with woe and at other times gave her the inspiration of her most amusing letters. To Mrs. Carlyle, life itself was absurd enough without inventing further absurdities. Mme de Sévigné in the construction of her *Lettre des foins* comes closest to the " pure bite " creators, Swift and Lamb, but only in so reasonable, classical and dignified a fashion that it is difficult to rank the two things together. There is a difference between exaggerated truth and nonsense. Mrs. Carlyle loved to be wayward in her representation of life, Mme de Sévigné loved to exaggerate, Swift and Lamb to invent, to lie, to make April fools of their friends, to indulge in any nonsense that might deceive for a moment, or even in nonsense too rank and outrageous ever to deceive anyone. This is a very old means of entertainment, a stock-in-trade of the court jester, studied and elaborated by Shakespeare. In Falstaff he created a past master in the refinements of this fundamentally simple and unsophisticated type of humour. With it often goes that most curious of intellectual tastes—the taste for punning. In cultured society there is no market for the childish ingenuity of puns, and it is natural that the majority of good letter-writers should have had little interest in them, being essentially members of such a society and sensitive to its conventions.

But Swift and Lamb were both men of peculiar individuality; they swam against the stream. Swift could be excellent company, but he could be vile company too. Lamb was charming, but he must have his joke at a funeral. When Mrs. Hood was delivered of a still-born child, Lamb wrote his beautiful lines " On an Infant Dying as soon as Born " and also wrote a note of sympathy to Hood, in which he told him that he had won " sexpence " from Moxon by guessing the sex of the infant. The reactions to social stimuli of Lamb or Swift could not be relied on; a contrary spirit dwelt within them and awoke when it was least welcome and least expected. With geniuses of this type humour may take strange forms, it may be, as with Lamb, one of the chief means which the spirit within has of expressing its contrariness. Swift undoubtedly found relaxation in fooling and punning. A heart which is lacerated with indignation does not find it amusing to observe human frailty and absurdity, and Mérimée (who did find it so) was not really a satirist or a misanthrope. Mérimée liked human nature just enough and not too much to find its pretences and its jealousies and stupidities good laughing matter when they took certain curious shapes—Walewski and the woman in Milan, or the devoted widow finding among her husband's papers love-letters in which the gender of both recipient and writer was masculine. When Swift relaxed he did not find his relaxation in such tales, but in absurdities that had as little relation as possible to actual life, in two hundred chapters of madness, in " pure bites," and bad puns. The trouble to which he and Lamb would go to deceive their friends is amazing to a modern person, for since Lamb's days the bite has become the monopoly of adolescents.

On March 31st Swift foregathered with Lady Masham and Dr. Arbuthnot for the purpose of contriving and spreading a circumstantial lie about a notorious criminal in order to catch as many April Fools as possible in one net. But best example of all in the *Journal to Stella* is the trick played upon the Bishop of Clogher. " If " puns were immensely in the vogue; Dillon Ashe murdered all his friends with them, and Swift himself would spend an evening making them up. In March 1713 the Bishop of Clogher made one so good—in his eyes—that he decided to send it to Ireland to his brother Tom. This was the pun: " If there was a hackney coach at Mr. Pooley's door, what town in Egypt would it be ? Hecatompolis; Hack at Tom Pooley's." Swift, however, forestalled the Bishop and got Sir Andrew Fountaine to write to Tom Ashe and tell him the pun and direct him to send it to the Bishop as his own; which he did. The ruse was successful, and the Bishop " sadly bit."

In Lamb we find greater variety, if not greater ingenuity than this. He indulged in a surprising number of different types of jokes. There is the leg-pull which raises a laugh because it is too obvious to pull any leg. " My faculties, thank God, are not much impaired. I have my sight, hearing, taste, pretty perfect; and can read the Lord's Prayer in the common type, by the help of a candle without making many mistakes."[1] His chief delight was to surprise, even if surprise could be achieved only by a mechanical arrangement of words, such as placing over the page the qualifying clause which made all the difference to his meaning. There is the joke—Shakespeare's, Falstaff's, and older—of the *non sequitur*. " For though the camomile, the more it is trodden on the faster it grows, yet youth, the more it is wasted the sooner it wears." At the end of Lamb's immortal description of a cold he says: " Yet do I try all I can to cure it, I try wine, and spirits, and smoking, and snuff in unsparing quantities, but they all only seem to make me worse, instead of better—I sleep in a damp room, but it does me no good: I come home late o' nights, but do not find any visible amendment."[2] He liked to surprise by recounting most shocking (but totally untrue)

[1] Lamb to Mr. and Mrs. J. D. Collier, January 6th, 1823.
[2] Lamb to Bernard Barton, January 9th, 1824.

calamities, and topping the tragedy—this is his impudence—with some commonplace particular that itself ridiculed the already ridiculous tragedy. Thus in the joint letter from himself and Mary to their child-friend Louisa Martin, Lamb says that a letter of his to Hazlitt from Bath was found inside Hazlitt's child at the post-mortem, together with a small hearth-brush and two golden pippins, after the child had died of swallowing a bag of white paint. " The letter," says Lamb, " had nothing remarkable in it."

To compare Lamb and Falstaff is of course absurd, but he has the Falstaffian flow of language and images, too ready to be merely an imitation,[1] and Falstaff's nimbleness in wit, the lightning changes from one side to another in his argument; above all things Falstaff's love of a hoax—" a bite, a palpable bite! "—and his gift for making himself the source of laughter. What Professor Bradley said truly of Falstaff is also true of Lamb : " Instead of being comic to you and serious to himself, he is more ludicrous to himself than to you; and he makes himself out more ludicrous than he is, in order that he and others may laugh."

Lamb liked to make himself out to be a perfect fool with strangers; after the first fiasco of a meeting with the blue-stocking Miss Benje he crowded cotton into his ears against the second meeting and read all the magazines and reviews in the hope of cutting " a

[1] Mr. E. V. Lucas suggests that Lamb may have had a hand in White's *Original Letters of Sir John Falstaff and his Friends*. If so, he early tried his hand at imitating the style of Shakespeare in the prose of *Henry IV*.

tolerable second-rate figure." Loquacious persons dismayed him and the self-satisfaction and lack of humour that generally accompany loquacity had the same effect upon him as the mock sorrow of a funeral party; he could not refrain from a pun or a joke. When the talkative gentleman who accompanied him and Emma Isola in the stage-coach from Epping to Enfield turned his discourse from Steam Engines and asked Lamb what he thought of the prospects of the turnip season, Lamb replied—to Emma Isola's delight—that he believed it depended very much on boiled legs of mutton. "We were rather less communicative, but still friendly, the rest of the way." Lamb probably always preferred to raise a laugh rather than to foster a conversation; there was something primitive and uncivilised in him.

But Lamb had also the capacity for a more sophisticated sort of humour. He was not a country recluse like Cowper, and although he lived in a very different circle from his contemporary Lady Bessborough,[1] he constantly met people and varieties of people. Lamb was a cockney and had the quick eye and the command of slang characteristic of the pure-bred cockney. See how he describes a man called Simonds who had tried to borrow money from him:

"Saving his dirty shirt and his physiognomy and his 'bacco box, together with a certain kiddy air in his walk, a man would have gone near to have mistaken

[1] But he "got drunk with claret and Tom Sheridan" in 1808 over a proposed collaboration in a pantomime, parts of which Tom and his father had already written.

him for a gentleman. He has a sort of ambition to be so misunderstood."[1]

This is not make-believe, but yet it is not Mrs. Carlyle's style of humour, or Mérimée's, or Cowper's. The misplacement of emphasis is a time-honoured cockney device for raising a laugh, and the eye that marked "a certain kiddy air in his walk" has the pitilessness of the London street urchin.

The quickness to see opportunities for frivolity and impudence towards the great was another urchin trait. In a letter to Wordsworth, Lamb recounts a conversation with a young man in his office who was "deep read in Anacreon, Moore, Lord Strangford, and the principal Modern Poets." "This" (the conversation which he has given between himself and the Young Gentleman) "led to an explanation (it could be delay'd no longer) that the sound Spencer, which when poetry is talk'd of generally excites an image of an old Bard in a Ruff, and sometimes with it dim notions of Sir P. Sydney and perhaps Lord Burleigh, had raised in my Gentleman a quite contrary image of The Honourable William Spencer, who has translated some things from the German very prettily, which are publish'd with Lady Di-Beauclerk's Designs."[2]

"An old Bard in a Ruff"—schoolboys have a natural propensity for such irreverence and feigned ignorance. Mary Lamb, so her brother informed Wordsworth, grew so weary of putting female characters into boys' clothes in the "Tales from Shakespeare"

[1] Lamb to John Rickman, Autumn 1801.
[2] Lamb to Wordsworth, January 1st, 1806.

that she began to think Shakespeare lacked imagination. "Dr. Harvey (who found out that blood was red) . . ." is in the same manner. An account of Shakespeare's muse in George Dyer's poems caused Lamb some surprise. "I thought she had been dead," he wrote to Manning, "and buried in Stratford Church, with the young man *that kept her company*. . . ." One can hardly imagine Lamb having Cowper's dream about Milton[1] without insinuating into it some prank or freak of impertinence that would have destroyed the exquisite tenor of the encounter.

While Swift's *Journal to Stella* is one of the most personal collections of letters in English, full of intimate foolishness, Lamb's letters are the least private of all letters. Lamb was amusing about people, customs, events. He was rarely amusing in his manner towards a person. While he wrote a great deal about himself and made endless copy out of himself, his character and his experiences, both in his essays and his letters, it was never the simple personal detail that makes up the *Journal to Stella*. It was all more detached, more sophisticated. Swift was quite unselfconscious, Lamb the very opposite. Without any desire to reveal himself, Swift makes even the discomfort of his troubled dreams as familiar to us as the discomfort of our own.

"(October) 14. (1710). Is that tobacco at the top of the paper, or what? I do not remember I slobbered. Lord, I dreamed of Stella etc. so confusedly last night, and that we saw Dean Bottom and Sterne go into a shop; and she bid me call them to her, and they proved

[1] See p. 137.

to be two parsons I knew not; and I walked without till she was shifting, and such stuff, mixed with much melancholy and uneasiness, and things not as they should be, and I know not how; and it is now an ugly gloomy morning."

Lamb, like Swift, is so familiar a part of our general ideas, so nearly a truism of the past, that we imagine everything must be known about him. But actually, Lamb is hard to know, even more so than Swift. We can form no conception of the kind of self he might have revealed in love letters, and since he was never separated from Mary Lamb except by her fits of madness we cannot now discover anything about the language of affection and familiarity which they may have used. Most of Lamb's friends were literary people and so much of his early correspondence consists of discussion word by word of early literary excursions that, as human documents, their value is as small as those of any specialist wrapped up in the technicalities of his work.

Moreover, Lamb became an essayist by profession, and he seldom forgot it. Often in his letters he started an idea, gave it a trial run, then caught it and put it in his tail pocket for future use. And in the real extemporising of his letters he practised the simulated extemporising of his essays. Sometimes it happened that having said a thing once in a letter, he could not repeat it when he tried to do so in an essay: he wrote to his friend Manning, who was in Canton, "I don't know why I have forborne writing so long. But it is such a forlorn hope to send a scrap of paper straggling over wide oceans." This could scarcely be improved upon, the most one could hope for would be repetition, but when Lamb came to write "Distant Correspondents" he could not recapture either the image or the phrasing. "The weary world of waters between us oppresses the imagination. It is difficult to conceive how a scrawl of mine should ever stretch across it."

Several of the essays are to be found foreshadowed in the letters and if the letters lack the elaborate allusiveness, the supreme fancy, the finished absurdity of the essays, they have sometimes a directness and spontaneity not always to be found in the corresponding essay. This double-harnessing of letter-writing and essay-writing became in Lamb's letters a literary preoccupation which puts them in a place apart. A born letter-writer—Walpole, Mme de Sévigné or even Fitzgerald—can be relied upon never to forget either himself or his correspondent, never to rhapsodise, never to concentrate too long or too fervently upon any subject. The manners of letter-writing are the manners of polite conversation, and in these Lamb continually defaults. The superiority of the town over the country strikes him, he remembers the charms of an actress or the flavour of a favourite dish, and he is off, absorbed and lost in his subject, and nothing will recall him until inspiration runs dry. In this as in his style of writing he is peculiarly masculine. The feminine mind is what Bacon called "bird-witted," its attention is the most mobile thing about it, and therefore the feminine mind, whether owned by a man or a woman, is excellently suited to letter-writing. Lamb was not by nature a letter-writer, he suited letter-writing to his own ends.

It is worth remembering that he disliked biographies. " What damn'd Unitarian skewer-soul'd things the general biographies turn out," he wrote, and clever as he was at making copy from his own life, he avoided disclosing his most personal feelings. What he said in letters to Wordsworth, Coleridge or Manning was seldom more intimate than what he said in his essays. Moreover, he had not much gift for reporting conversations or gossip; he was sociable indeed at times, but with the worker's hatred of people as constituting interruptions to the real business of life. " Evening Company I should always like had I any mornings, but I am saturated with human faces (*divine* forsooth) and voices all the golden morning. . . . I am never C. L. but always C. L. and Co." . . . His humorous references to the trials of friendship had sometimes a sub-acidity even more forcible than Swift's plain cynicism upon the constancy of his enemies.

" Never any poor devil was so befriended as I am. Do you know any poor solitary human that wants that cordial to life—a true friend ? I can spare him twenty, he shall have 'em good cheap. I have gallipots of 'em—genuine balm of cares—a going—a going—a going."[1]

Lamb had no illusions about human nature, even at twenty-one when he dealt with " the old hag of a wealthy relation " whom he describes in a letter to Coleridge.[2] When George Dyer was starving, Lamb

[1] Lamb to Coleridge, July 2nd, 1825.
[2] *Ditto*, December 9th, 1796.

was exceedingly kind to him, but the letter to John Rickman describing how Dyer was rescued is perfectly unsentimental and plain spoken. " I shall not be sorry when he takes his nipt carcase out of my bed, which it has occupied, and vanishes with all his Lyric lumber, but I will endeavour to bring him in future into a method of dining at least once a day."[1] He was never ashamed to admit that there were limits to his patience and kindliness. The " stupid big country wench " who came to the Lambs as a maid in 1810 and fell ill, lay in bed—" a dead weight upon our humanity," said Lamb. Fops and pretenders received little mercy from his hands, and the amateurs in literature who pestered him with their questions were slaughtered outright. " They had," he said to Mrs. Wordsworth, " the form of reading men, but, for any possible use Reading can be to them but to talk of, might as well have been Ante-Cadmeans born, or have lain sucking out the sense of an Egyptian hieroglyph as long as the Pyramids will last before they should find it."[2]

The universe at large he regarded with some irony. After launching a hoax letter on Crabb Robinson to make fun of his rheumatic agonies, he lets his sharpest arrow fly at much bigger game. " Well, it is not in my method to inflict pangs. I leave that to heaven." At another time when afflicted with " a dulling cold " he expressed himself more mildly—" My theory is to enjoy life, but the practice is against it." " Saint

[1] Lamb to John Rickman, November 1801.
[2] Lamb to Mrs. Wordsworth, February 1818.

Charles" was the nickname he afterwards earned, but few saints have dared to be so frankly materially minded. He wished he were rich and would not care if it meant being "squeezed camel-fashion at getting through that needle's eye." He feared that if he lived with Coleridge and Wordsworth he would lose his own commonplace identity; if he got "within the whiff and wind" of Coleridge's genius he could scarcely possess his soul in quiet. It was matter for self-congratulation that in the East India office there was less metaphysics in thirty-six of his companions than in the first page of Locke *On the Human Understanding*, "or as much poetry in any ten lines of the Pleasures of Hope or more natural Beggar's Petition." When Bernard Barton wrote to him saying that he wanted to give up his place in a bank for the sake of writing, Lamb replied in the most unequivocal terms, advising him not to be so rash and warning him against the Turks and Tartars that are booksellers (we should say publishers to-day). "In my inner heart do I approve and embrace this our close but unharassing way of life." His attitude to Manning was typically insular—Manning who, wearing a beard of remarkable length, carried brass candlesticks and Nankin tea and English lavender water to the Grand Llama, at that time (1811) a boy of seven, and was the first Englishman allowed inside the gates of Lhasa. Lamb had done his best to persuade Manning from going to China—"The Tartars, really, are a cold, insipid, smouchy set." Manning might expect to be eaten and have "the cool malignity of mustard and vinegar" added to the dish. Of himself Lamb said with a good deal of truth that he was a Christian, Englishman, Londoner, Templar, and had a timid imagination that disliked anything remote or strange either in space or thought. He could "just endure Moors, because of their connection as foes with Christians."

Lamb was town bred and a town dweller. He belonged more to the nineteenth than to the eighteenth century. Cowper at Olney, Gray at Cambridge, Walpole and Swift in their small eighteenth-century worlds did not have the same need to underline their individuality. In the country or in a small familiar group of people the individual has little struggle to assert himself. But in cities and as population increases, a superficial similarity clothes men and women, and it requires either gross or courageous egotism for one man in a community of millions to believe in his distinction and to assert it. Except in rare cases it also requires some skill, the ability to frame a thesis about oneself and to make that thesis intelligible to strangers. All sorts of exaggerations and absurdities are committed by people sensitive to social codes and determined at all costs not to be mistaken for anyone else. Lamb was one of the first people to realise the necessity of emphasising all the points upon which he differed from other people. His essay-writing stimulated him to emphasise them still more, and he allowed his professional manner to permeate his private life—either that, or he elaborated his private manner for professional ends. Lady Bessborough or Gray would not have thought it good style to make so much of personal idiosyncrasies.

As Lamb distinguished himself, so he distinguishes his friends. He picked out characteristics that identified them for ever beyond fear of confusion. "What is gone of that frank-hearted circle, Morgan and his cos lettuces? He ate walnuts better than any man I ever knew." Then there was Marshall: "That Bitch [Mrs Godwin] has detached Marshall from his house, Marshall the man who went to sleep when the 'Ancient Mariner' was reading." He established Godwin's uniqueness by telling him to his face that he had read more books that weren't worth reading than any man in England.

When Lamb turned his attention from his friends to those he disliked, his capacity for exaggeration gathered strength and brilliance and the infusion of acid grew more marked.

"I forgot to tell you," he wrote to Landor in October 1832, "I knew all your Welch annoyances, the measureless Beethams—I knew a quarter of a mile of them. 17 brothers and 16 sisters, as they appear to me in memory. There was one of them that used to fix his long legs on my fender, and tell a story of a shark, every night, endless, immortal. How have I grudged the salt sea ravener not having had his gorge of him!

"The shortest of the daughters measured 5 foot eleven without her shoes. Well, some day we may confer about them. But they were tall. Surely I have discover'd the longitude. . . ."

But no one doubts that Lamb's ferocity about the Beethams behind their backs was redeemed by mildness and courtesy to their faces. Lamb rode in the van of the crusade against bores, but in his case as in so many others the crusade turned into a martyrdom. The greater the bore the greater his invulnerability, and in making proof of the enemy's imperviousness the assailant must often suffer the last extremities of boredom. The envy, perfidy and ambition of the early eighteenth century created conflicts that were real and bloody, but the divisions between Swift and other men were never so profound as those which Lamb makes between himself and a quarter-mile of Beethams, or Mrs. Carlyle between herself and an American. The snobbishness of individuality, while much more entertaining to practice and observe than class or intellectual snobbishness, has less compatibility with democracy than either of them. It blots out of the book of life hordes of human beings.

So Lamb dealt with people, far more subtly than Walpole did in his letter-chronicles, while still looking upon the world as consisting of people and dominated by people, just as Walpole had looked upon it. To neither of them did it occur that the mind could be more fittingly occupied than in the pleasure-duty of reducing the mob of humanity to some order, whether by narrative and description, or by putting a finger upon the significant idiosyncrasy—" He ate walnuts better than any man I ever knew "—or by proscription. Lady Bessborough, Cowper, Dorothy Osborne, were too taken up with their private relationships to share this attitude, but whether or not we divide letter-writers into two groups, according as their interest was general or personal, the object of that interest does not vary. Personality is the central theme of the two centuries from Dorothy Osborne and Mme de Sévigné to Mrs. Carlyle and Mérimée. No doubt men and women in the Dark Ages and the Renascence loved and hated as deeply as they have in subsequent ages, but their love and hatred for one another flowed beneath the sand, and the story of individual lives comes down to us only through the institutions which they built, the causes for which they fought, and the careers of those princes to whom they swore allegiance. With the seventeenth century, as has often been pointed out, the power and dominance of princes and institutions began to shrink, and the idea of the individual life as *chose grave* was born.

We think of it in this way now, but in vastly different circumstances. Just as the Church and other tyrannies once towered over Europe, so War and Economics now tower over the world. Periodically humanity sets in motion a train of events too complicated and too powerful for it to control or even to understand, and all that people care for most goes to the wall; wisdom fails from the earth when fear is at its roots. These ten letter-writers lived in a time of ease and confidence. Walpole may have dreaded sneers, Mme du Deffand boredom, Lady Bessborough and Mme de Sévigné misfortune to those they loved, and Cowper, who suffered the most, feared damnation; none was perfectly happy, for no human being of intelligence has ever been perfectly happy, but they lived on the whole tranquilly, in a world where only the poor starved, and soldiers only were killed in war. In their dreams of the future men might fly like birds, but they could scarcely foresee the possibility of a famine accompanied by too much wheat or guess to what lengths that " illiberal manner " of conducting wars, so deplored by Lady Bessborough, might be carried.

Life in the eighteenth century may have been far from perfect, but to remove most of its imperfections lay within the power of man. Indeed those imperfections have been largely remedied, its prisons and madhouses, its dirt and ignorance; but the perfections too have gone. It is far too soon to gauge the full effect upon literature of so great a change as this. Human nature quickly adapts itself to living in dread and misery, and poetry builds its nest even in the cannon's mouth. But the genius for poetry is a sturdier and more persistent thing than the genius for letters: the detachment of the good letter-writer, his absorption in personal and domestic affairs, is something which may never be recaptured. The twentieth century is neither serene nor secure; indeed, in spite of postmen and modern education, it is scarcely more conducive than the fifteenth to the writing of what Lady Bessborough called " comfortable letters." If we could examine the post-bag of the world to-day its characteristic letters might prove to be as laconic as the Pastons', asking for a necklace, accounting for money spent, telling of illness and misfortune.

APPENDIX

AND

INDEX

APPENDIX (See page 128)

"You possibly remember that at a place called Weston, little more than a mile from Olney, there lives a family whose name is Throckmorton. The present possessor of the estate is a young man whom I remember as a boy. He has a wife, who is young, genteel, and handsome. They are Papists, but much more amiable than many Protestants. We never had any intercourse with the family, though ever since we lived here we have enjoyed the range of their pleasure grounds, having been favoured with a key, which admits us into all. When this man succeeded to the estate, on the death of his elder brother, and came to settle at Weston, I sent him a complimentary card, requesting the continuance of that privilege, having till then enjoyed it by the favour of his mother, who on that occasion went to finish her days at Bath. You may conclude that he granted it, and for about two years nothing more passed between us. A fortnight ago, I received an invitation in the civilest terms, in which he told me that the next day he should attempt to fill a balloon, and if it would be any pleasure to me to be present, should be happy to see me. Your mother and

I went. The whole country was there, but the balloon could not be filled. The endeavour was, I believe, very philosophically made, but such a process depends for its success upon such niceties as make it very precarious. Our reception was, however, flattering to a great degree, insomuch that more notice seemed to be taken of us than we could possibly have expected; indeed rather more than of any of his other guests. They even seem anxious to recommend themselves to our regards. We drank chocolate, and were asked to dine, but were engaged. A day or two afterwards, Mrs. Unwin and I walked that way, and were overtaken in a shower. I found a tree that I thought would shelter us both—a large elm, in a grove that fronts the mansion. Mrs. T. observed us, and running towards us in the rain insisted on our walking in. He was gone out. We sat chatting with her till the weather cleared up, and then at her instance took a walk with her in the garden. The garden is almost their only walk, and is certainly their only retreat in which they are not liable to interruption. She offered us a key of it in a manner that made it impossible not to accept it, and said she would send us one. A few days afterwards, in the cool of the evening, we walked that way again. We saw them going toward the house, and exchanged bows and curtsies at a little distance, but did not join them. In a few minutes, when we had passed the house, and had almost reached the gate that opens out of the park into the adjoining field, I heard the iron gate belonging to the court-yard ring, and saw Mr. T. advancing hastily toward us; we made equal haste to meet him, he presented to us the key, which I told him I esteemed a singular favour, and after a few such speeches as are made on such occasions, we parted. This happened about a week ago. I concluded nothing less than that all this civility and attention was designed, on their part, as a prelude to a nearer acquaintance; but here at present the matter rests. I should like exceedingly to be on an easy footing there, to give a morning call, and now and then to receive one, but nothing more. For though he is one of the most agreeable men I ever saw, I could not wish to visit him in any other way, neither our house, furniture, servants, or income being such as qualify us to make entertainments; neither would I on any account be introduced to the neighbouring gentry, which must be the consequence of our dining there; there not being a man in the country, except himself, with whom I could endure to associate. They are squires, merely such, purse-proud and sportsmen. But Mr. T. is altogether a man of fashion, and respectable on every account."[1]

[1] William Cowper to William Unwin, May 1784.

INDEX

INDEX

INDEX